July 5, 2006

Ryan

Congratulations
on becoming a pitcher for
the Cincinnati Reds —
wishing you continued
Success!

Renie & Bill

D0891936

Tom Browning's

TALES FROM THE
REDS
DUGOUT

Tom Browning
with Dann Stupp

Foreword by Joe Nuxhall

SPORTS
PUBLISHING
L.L.C.

SportsPublishingLLC.com

Publishers: Peter L. Bannon and Joseph J. Bannon Sr.
Senior managing editor: Susan M. Moyer
Acquisitions editor: Joseph J. Bannon Jr.
Developmental editor: Elisa Bock Laird
Art director: K. Jeffrey Higgerson
Dust jacket design: Joseph Brumleve
Interior layout: Kathryn R. Holleman
Photo editor: Erin Linden-Levy

Printed in the United States of America

Sports Publishing L.L.C.
804 North Neil Street
Champaign, IL 61820
Phone: 1-877-424-2665
Fax: 217-363-2073
SportsPublishingLLC.com

Library of Congress Cataloging-in-Publication Data

Browning, Tom, 1960-
    [Tales from the Reds dugout]
    Tom Browning's tales from the Reds dugout / Tom Browning with Dann
Stupp ; foreword, Joe Nuxhall.
        p. cm.
    ISBN 1-59670-046-7 (hardcover : alk. paper)
    1. Cincinnati Reds (Baseball team) I. Title: Tales from the Reds dugout. II.
Stupp, Dann, 1978- III. Title.

GV875.C65B76 2006
796.357'640977178—dc22

                             2006002278

I dedicate this book to all of the teammates I had the privilege of playing with. Each and every one of you had a bearing on my career as well as my life. I thank you for your camaraderie and friendship. I love telling the stories of the past. I hope that you will enjoy reading some of them. To my 1990 World Series champion teammates, thank you for "the ring, the money, everything." —T.B.

To my folks, who engrained in me a love of a baseball and a passion for writing. Your support and encouragement still amaze me. —D.S.

CONTENTS

FOREWORD

During my 60-plus years as a Reds player and broadcaster, I've seen many all types of guys come and go from the Cincinnati dugout. But Tom Browning, our newest Reds Hall of Famer, remains in a class all his own.

When you look through the long and storied history of the Cincinnati Reds, the oldest team in professional baseball, you find just one perfect game. Watching Tom pitch that night remains one of my favorite Reds memories. In fact, I was so excited to talk to him after that historic performance that I nearly knocked myself unconscious to get the interview (skip ahead to Chapter 7 for the full story).

Tom, however, is more than just that perfect game. From my perch in the press box, I watched a bulldog of a pitcher challenge hitter after hitter, year after year. I loved Tom's mentality and intensity. He always wanted the ball. He wanted to go after the hitter, and he didn't back down from anyone.

However, as intense as Tom was on the mound, he was about as freewheeling and carefree as you could get off the field. He was a guy who liked to have fun, and that's a big reason we became such great friends. And it's also a reason the following pages will be such a memorable journey through Reds baseball.

I hope you enjoy reading Tom's tales as much as I enjoyed being a part of them.

–Joe Nuxhall

ACKNOWLEDGMENTS

Many thanks to the fine folks at Sports Publishing L.L.C for making this book a reality, specifically Elisa Bock Laird, Joe Bannon Jr., and Erin Linden-Levy. We would also like to thank the Cincinnati Reds, specifically John Allen and Ralph Mitchell, for signing off on the project and lending their support. A big thanks to Jarrod Rollins for the invaluable feedback, as well as Jansen Dell and the rest of the Reds Creative Services department.

We are also appreciative of the following individuals for a variety of reasons: Todd Benzinger, Kathryn Braun, Marty Brennaman, Debbie Browning, Jerry Dowling, Chris Eckes, Charley Frank, Jenny Gardner, Rich Gibson, Amy Hafer, Brian Hunterman, Jeff Idelson, Russ Jenisch, Laura Kellison, Joe Nuxhall, Ronnie Oester, Greg Rhodes, Ronald Roth, Glenn Sample, Dave Storm, Mark Stowe, and Rick Stowe. And finally, our thanks to the individuals behind www.retrosheet.org and www.baseball-reference.com for the wonderful resources they provide.

THE PRIDE OF WYOMING

DESTINATION: CINCINNATI

From the earliest age, I just knew I was going to be a professional ballplayer. I never really considered another career option.

Even to this day, I never think about what it would have been like if I had fallen short of my big league dreams. I simply accepted that baseball was going to be my future.

Maybe it was an unexplained confidence in my abilities, or maybe I was just too stubborn to give up. Regardless, I knew I'd do whatever it would take to get to the majors.

That's not to say the journey was an easy one. Although I always enjoyed playing baseball, it never came easy. I couldn't rely on natural talent—because I just didn't have much of it. I wasn't the hardest thrower, the fastest runner, or the most gifted athlete. But I had a solid and durable arm, and I worked hard. I made the most of my abilities, and I never took an opportunity for granted.

With some perseverance, I knew I would someday be playing with the best in baseball. I wouldn't necessarily be the best, but I knew I could at least compete with the best.

I just knew I wanted to play on baseball's biggest stage, and I wanted to do it in a Cincinnati uniform.

PINHEAD FRIENDS

It's hard for many people to believe that a kid from Casper, Wyoming, could become such a diehard Reds fan.

It actually started with a bowling league. A lot of my friends were in the league, and we bowled on Saturday mornings. It'd be 11 a.m. in Casper. That was the time that the MLB *Game of the Week* came on. They had all of the televisions in the bowling alley tuned in.

This was around 1970, right about the time the Big Red Machine started taking shape, and Reds games were aired pretty often.

Our bowling league started up after school was back in session, so we're talking about the fall, when the pennant races were really heating up. Between my turns bowling, I was fixed to the screen.

I became a huge fan of guys like Tony Perez, Johnny Bench, and Dave Concepcion. As a baseball fan, I was captivated by the team. They were just so good, and they made it look so easy. However, they just couldn't seem to get over the hump and win the World Series.

I was hooked anyway.

I think I was the only one who really cared about the Reds back then. Most of my buddies were A's fans. They always talked about guys like Catfish Hunter, Vida Blue, and Reggie Jackson. We didn't have any major league teams around us, so we could pretty much pick any team to root for. And at that time, Oakland was every bit as good as Cincinnati.

My friends gave me all kinds of crap for being a Reds fan. It was nonstop. It was good-natured ribbing, but it only made me like the Reds even more. It felt like it was really my team.

Right before my freshman year of high school, my two brothers, two sisters, and I moved with my mom and stepfather to a small town near Utica, New York. By that time, the Reds were really coming into their own. They'd soon win four pennants in seven seasons and back-to-back World Series titles in 1975 and 1976.

The only downside to Cincinnati's success was not being around those A's fans. It sure would have been nice to rub it in.

SPORTS BUMS

My mom always worried that she was raising a family of baseball, basketball, and football junkies—"sports bums," as she called it.

She was a tough, but loving mom. She had the five of us kids before she turned 21, and she was the primary caretaker and disciplinarian. She tried to limit the amount of sports we watched on television, but she was fighting a losing battle. We loved everything sports related.

As far back as I can remember, my dad and uncles played competitive fast-pitch softball. This wasn't like the beer leagues you see today with a bunch of fat guys running around. The games were dominated by pitching, and it was about as close as you could get to playing real baseball.

My dad went all over the state for games and tournaments. He was gone a lot, and I'm sure it played a part in my parents' divorce when I was seven. That's probably why my mom worried when she was saw us following in his footsteps.

However, once she realized I was serious about following my dream and might actually have the talent to do it, she couldn't have been more supportive.

Once I started playing professionally, she came to games as often as she could, and she taped many more. She was one of my biggest supporters, and I loved her dearly for it.

It's sort of a big league tradition to buy your mom a new house when you sign your first big contract. Once I got to Cincinnati, I got to do the same. It was one of the most rewarding parts of becoming a major leaguer.

QUICK WORKER

Throughout my major league career, I was known for working quickly. I didn't like to spend a lot of time fiddling around between pitches. I got the ball, and I threw the ball. It was all about rhythm.

I probably picked it up from my dad's softball games. They played seven innings, and the games were on a time limit of 75 minutes. My dad was a pitcher, and he worked quickly so they could get all of the games in. I just assumed that was the natural flow of the game.

Even in Little League, I worked quickly. A poor kid could barely get his foot in the batter's box before I fired a pitch. I always thought it was funny when I had nine and 10 year olds stepping out of the box to slow me down.

CASPER'S FIRST FAMILY

All of my brothers, sisters, and cousins played baseball with me.

The Brownings were kind of the first family of sports in Casper. My dad and uncles were some of the best amateur softball players around.

Even the girls were good. My cousin Denae broke our league's record for home runs, one that had been held by Mike Lansing, who hit 20 home runs for the 1997 Montreal Expos. I remember my sister playing senior Little League with us and getting six hits in her first 10 at-bats. Even my grandmother, Lolita, was an All-America basketball player back in her day.

My brother Bill and I were probably the most competitive in the family. Bill, who was a year older than me, was a great shortstop. We had an awesome pickoff move. We got everybody out with it. When I was pitching, I didn't even worry about runners on first. I just waited for them to get to second, and then Bill and I would pick them off.

My other love was basketball. I played it in high school and even on a team that the Reds put together in the offseason, but it all started back home. Casper is 7,000 feet above sea level, so it snowed all the time. Bill and I would shovel the driveway as fast as we could so that we could get out and play.

We had absolute battles out there. I was a little taller than Bill, but even though he was my older brother, he wouldn't budge an inch. He made me earn every single bucket. There were plenty of times when we returned with busted lips or bruises from our wars.

I loved the competition and being pushed like that. I knew it made me a better athlete.

Once I made the majors, I always thought I could go the distance for the complete game. I hated to be pulled from a game. They called me a bulldog, and I'm sure it was those one-on-one battles with Bill that helped make me that way.

CHARLIE HUSTLE COMES TO CASPER

It wasn't so much the fame or money that made me want to play ball professionally. I just loved playing the game.

The one part that really did appeal to me was knowing that I could be playing with the best. You could only do that in the majors.

I think it probably started as a 10-year-old, when our baseball league flew in Johnny Bench for our year-end banquet. Imagine it. Johnny

Bench, a major league All-Star—in Casper, Wyoming, a place that couldn't be farther off the baseball map. As a 10-year-old, I thought it was quite the treat.

Johnny was great. He gave a nice little speech and then signed autographs for all of the kids. I remember waiting in line and looking at this huge ring he had on his hand. It must have been the size of a golf ball, with what seemed like hundreds of diamonds in it. His hand gave off a huge shimmer every time he signed an autograph.

It wasn't too unusual for players to take gigs like that back then. They were making good money at the time, but nothing like players make today, so the guys didn't mind doing odd events for a small fee.

The next year we flew in Reggie Jackson, who was a big hit for all of the Oakland fans.

Then, to top it off, we flew in Pete Rose the following year. I was always a Pete fan. I loved the way he played the game. I had never seen anyone so intense or play so hard. I just felt like anything could happen when he was in the game.

Pete captivated his audiences, and our banquet was no different. Even the A's fans were excited to see him.

I don't remember the exact details of his short speech that night, but I remember the main theme. It was something about playing as hard as you can and never giving up on your dreams. It couldn't have been more fitting for a guy like me.

Pete was saying exactly what I wanted to hear, and I soon realized he and I had a lot in common. Like me, I'm sure Pete never even considered what he would do if baseball hadn't worked out for him. He had committed himself to playing ball and wouldn't take no for an answer.

It was only fitting that a guy like Pete was the first person to welcome me to my first major league clubhouse 12 years later.

WYOMING PRIDE

Back in 1999, *Sports Illustrated* released its list of the top 50 athletes from each state. Mixed in with the rodeo bareback riding champions, Olympic discus throwers, and junior cross-country skiers was my name, fifth overall on the list for Wyoming. The list included a handful of other major leaguers, including Mike Lansing and Mike Devereaux.

It was a real honor seeing my name in the magazine, because I've always taken great pride in where I come from.

People have often asked me if I consider being from such a remote place a disadvantage when it came to baseball. Granted, we weren't exactly a metropolis, but we weren't some backwoods hick-town either. We had running water, electricity, and even a Burger King.

We also had very competitive sports leagues, ones that played an important role in developing me into a ballplayer.

When we first left Wyoming and moved to New York, I hated it. They all talked funny, wore "sneakers," and drank "soda." It was like they were speaking a foreign language.

But New York also had baseball and basketball leagues, and that's all I really needed as a kid.

2

GETTING NOTICED

READY TO COMPETE

O nce we moved to New York, I played my first two years of high school ball at Chadwicks High in Utica and then after my stepfather got transferred, my final two years at Franklin Academy in Malone.

I pitched and played center field. I loved playing center. Center was my first love, but I didn't have the speed or the bat to make it past high school, so I enjoyed it while I could. I loved the idea of playing every day and getting to hit, and even in the majors, I missed that aspect of the game.

Pitching was my calling card, though. I hadn't grown into my body yet, and I weighed just 155 pounds when I graduated from high school. I wasn't that strong and didn't have a lot on my pitches, but even then I knew how to pitch and hit my marks and change speeds. And I was a durable pitcher, and I knew that was important.

During my senior year of high school, I pitched 13 innings in an extra-inning tournament quarterfinal game, played center field the next day, and then threw seven more innings the day after that. We weren't really too concerned about pitch counts back then, and besides, I just wanted to compete and try to win. To me, that was most important.

Back in high school, I had aspirations of being a center fielder, but I knew pitching would be my ticket to the bigs. *Photo courtesy of Tom Browning*

ANDY VAN "SLICK"

Before my junior and senior years of high school, I played summer Legion ball with Andy Van Slyke in Utica. If there were any potential major leaguers around me, "Slick" was surely it. He made everything he did look easy.

We had some good players on those teams, but Andy was far and away the star. He had already found his talent, and he had one of the sweetest swings I had ever seen. There was no question whether he'd make it to the pros. The only question was how good he would end up being.

The guy could do anything and play anywhere. And he looked good doing it. He played first and third for us. He could also catch. And next to Eric Davis, he was the best center fielder I ever saw play the game.

Andy was a first-round pick in the 1979 draft, taken by the St. Louis Cardinals when he was just 18 years old. By his 22nd birthday, he was promoted to the major league club, where Whitey Herzog used him at three or four different positions. He was traded to Pittsburgh a few years later and won something like five straight Gold Gloves. Jimmy Leyland ended up moving Barry Bonds to left field just because Andy was so good in center.

I think the key to Andy's success was his "major league mentality." He developed it early in life. He had the raw talent and the drive, but he also had that aura of cockiness and arrogance that every good ballplayer seems to have.

Andy knew he had the talent, and he knew he'd only have himself to blame if he never made it.

Even in the majors, I saw guys who had the talent, but didn't have the drive or confidence to make the most of it. It was such a shame. I just couldn't relate. I would have done anything for the natural talent some of those guys had, but they just pissed it away. Andy, though, was the best of both worlds.

A BAD BREAK

A broken arm eventually cut short my career in 1995. But it was a different break on my non-pitching arm that nearly ended my professional career before it ever began.

After my senior year of high school, I decided to go back to Wyoming to spend some time with my dad. I got permission to play with my old Legion team that summer. I had committed to play college ball in the fall, so I wanted to stay sharp, and I knew the league was plenty competitive.

To earn some money that summer, I took a job my uncle had arranged at the True Oil Company in Casper. I helped unload huge 1,200-pound pipes from a forklift. One guy would drive them over to me, and then I would cut a bundle loose and let them roll down the forklift's arms into a storage area.

It was a Friday, and we were freeing the last bundle of the week. As I tried to release the pipes, they broke loose and crashed to the ground.

Andy Van Slyke and I catch up on old times before a Reds-Cardinals game. "Slick" was one of the area's top prospects when we were in high school back in New York.
Photo courtesy of Tom Browning

Unfortunately, they were spring-loaded, and one of them shot up from the ground and punctured my right forearm. The pain hit me instantly, and it was sickening. My arm was completely mangled, and the forearm bent like I had another elbow.

They rushed me to the hospital. At first, the doctors weren't even sure they'd be able to save the arm because it was in such bad shape. It didn't even look like an arm, just a mess of skin, blood, and bones hanging from my elbow.

I was stupid. It never even occurred that this could have been the end of my baseball dreams. Somehow, even if I lost the arm, I would find a way to make it to the majors, I thought.

Eventually, they fixed me up with a metal plate and some screws. I still have scars on that arm where it looks like they had to butterfly me open to straighten it all out.

The plate didn't come out for a year, and I missed all of the fall baseball season while I was in a cast. But I realized how lucky I was. It'd take some healing, but I knew I'd pitch again. It was just going to take some patience.

ROAD TRIP

Knowing I was feeling depressed about my broken arm, my good friend Mark Pepin wanted to do something to cheer me up when I got back to New York.

He checked the Reds schedule and saw that they were going to be playing in Montreal, which was a short drive from Malone.

Believe it or not, I was 18 years old and had never been to a major league game before. Yes, I had a deprived childhood. Actually, my family had made a few trips to see the minor league Denver Bears when I was younger, but it wasn't the same thing.

For those excursions, all seven of us piled into a Volkswagen bug for six or seven hours. There were four of us in the backseat, the youngest on my mom's lap, and Dad in the driver's seat. We didn't complain, though, because those trips were always something to look forward to.

On our trip to Montreal Mark and I drove to Olympic Stadium and scalped some cheap tickets. Even though it was indoors, had artificial turf, and was hardly a stadium at all, the place blew me away. I was so amazed by the entire atmosphere.

I was most excited when I saw the Cincinnati Reds take the field. The starting lineup contained a virtual who's who of Reds legends: Pete Rose, Joe Morgan, George Foster, Dan Driessen, Johnny Bench, and Dave Concecpion, with Tom Seaver on the mound.

I forgot all about my arm because I was just so awestruck. Every ball sounded like it was crushed, and every pitch looked like it was going 150 miles per hour. In the first inning, Foster connected on a pitch.

"It's gone, Mark!" I shouted. "It's gone!"

I hadn't exactly mastered the art of tracking flight paths. The ball never got past second base. Mark just laughed at me.

But I couldn't have asked for a more exciting game. Pete led off the sixth inning with a single to extend his hitting streak to 36 games. (He would later break the National League record with 44 straight.) The game was tied 4-4 and went into extra innings. As the 30,000 or so fans trickled out of the stadium, Mark and I moved closer and closer to the field.

After nearly five hours and 14 innings, Pete launched a ball to right field, a sacrifice fly that put the Reds up 5-4. Pedro Borbon closed out the bottom of the inning, and Cincinnati won my first big league game.

Mark and I worked our way down to the Reds dugout right after the last out. I wanted to see if we could get a peek at any of the guys. It was mostly empty by then, but then one guy in the dugout started walking right toward us.

"Great game, Mr. Rose," I said.

Pete smiled, thanked us, and then gave us a small toast with his can of Orange Crush.

As far as baseball memories, that's one of my favorites.

ME AND J.D.

One of the best friends I ever made in baseball was Jim Deshaies, a former Houston pitcher and now a TV broadcaster for the Astros. He and his wife, Lori, are still very close to my family. But back in high school, I couldn't have had a more bitter rival.

When we played Massena Central High, Jimmy was the guy to keep an eye on. He was intimidating as a pitcher in high school because he was so big and threw so damn hard. He had major league written all over him—a big powerful lefty who could just pound the strike zone with rising fastballs that scared everyone.

Jimmy had me in his back pocket. I couldn't hit a lefty to save my life, especially one who threw that hard.

My favorite memory of Jimmy actually came from the basketball court. We both played in high school, and we were at his school for a varsity game. Our team was shafted by the refs that night—a real "homer" job. Late in the game, I was trying to grab a rebound, and one of their guys came over top my back, bending me in half to get to the ball. We both fell to the floor, and unbelievably, they called the foul on me. It was my fifth, so I was out. Fuming, I gave their guy a foot to the ribs. It wasn't

Once teammates at LeMoyne College, Jimmy Deshaies and I found each other on opposite sides of the lines in the majors. *Photo courtesy of the Cincinnati Reds*

really a kick, just kind of a push with my foot to let him know I was fed up.

Jimmy was on the court and saw the whole thing, and he looked at me like he was ready to kill me. The guy always looked intimidating back then.

"In the spring, it's gonna be in your ear," he said to me.

He was referring to my next at-bat against him once the baseball season started.

Needless to say, I didn't have to worry about getting a hit off him once that day came. If he was pitching that spring, I was standing nowhere near the plate.

After high school, we both got offers to play ball at LeMoyne College, a small school in Syracuse, New York, which had a great baseball program. Jimmy and I soon became great friends and learned we had a lot in common. We even helped LeMoyne to two Division II College World Series appearances.

ROCK-SOLID ADVICE

Once I was on the field, I was my own general. I knew what it took to win, and I usually didn't need much direction. My future was in my own hands.

However, a few key people always made sure I was headed in the right direction. Dick Rockwell, my coach at LeMoyne College, was one of them. He genuinely cared about his players, and I think he saw some promise in me. So he pulled me aside one day during my freshman year to offer some words of wisdom.

"Look, you're a talented kid," he told me. "But if you want to play this game for a living, you're going to have to take things more seriously, especially your commitments off the field."

I appreciated his advice, and it meant a lot to me that he wanted me to succeed. I was drinking a lot of beer and partying a lot at the time. And although I probably didn't heed his advice like I should have sometimes, I got turned around and headed in the right direction.

In the following years, I noticed that all of my good managers and coaches had a similar approach. They knew that all kinds of success on the field didn't mean anything if you were a failure off the field, and they tried hard to keep you on the right path.

STRIKING OUT IN 1981

I didn't play all four years at LeMoyne College. I was so hell-bent on making the pros that I often let my grades slide. I was told that I would need to go to summer school to keep my eligibility after my junior year, so I decided instead to go to Virginia to play in the Shenandoah Valley League, a sort of Cape Cod League for rednecks. All of the Southern schools sent their best players there. John Kruk and Dan Pasqua, both future majors leaguers, were there, so it was a definitely a competitive league.

Although I had never met any scouts personally, I was hearing that there was a pretty good chance I was going to get drafted. A lot of people were comparing me to another pitcher near Malone named John Cerutti, who the Blue Jays ended up taking in the first round that year.

I decided the summer league would be my best opportunity to get noticed, too. Unfortunately, my timing couldn't have been any worse.

Major League Baseball went on strike that summer, and nearly a third of the season was lost.

For the Reds, it meant one of the worst snubs in baseball history. The league ended up using a weird split-season format to decide who would go to the playoffs, and despite having the best overall record in baseball, the Reds finished second in each half and were kept out of the postseason.

For me, it meant I needed a new plan. Because of the strike, teams weren't really looking to sign anyone. I had taken a gamble by leaving LeMoyne, and it had backfired.

Luckily, things turned out okay for me. One of my coaches in the summer league knew Rod Fridley, the head coach at Tennessee Wesleyan. It was a small school in Athens, Tennessee, but they played against some SEC powerhouses. Coach Fridley gave me a spot on the team, stuck me in his rotation, and gave me every opportunity to succeed. Looking back, it was probably one of the biggest breaks I got.

BEING SEEN

I just wasn't anything special, as far as baseball prospects go, anyway.

Back in college, my fastball probably maxed out at about 92 miles per hour. It was a respectable number, but it didn't exactly have scouts beating down my door. However, I always made sure to put myself in as many places as I could to be seen.

As it turned out, playing for Tennessee Wesleyan turned out to be one of those key places.

My biggest start for Wesleyan came early in the spring of 1982 against the University of Kentucky. As a senior, it was do-or-die time. I needed to get noticed soon if I wanted to be drafted.

On their way to a weekend series against the University of Tennessee, UK stopped by our place for a Thursday game, and I got the start.

Kentucky had a big Division I program that had some real hitters, but our little NAIA team squeaked out a win. And I shut them down. I must have struck out 15 Wildcats.

As it turned out, Kentucky's coach, Keith Madison, was a birddog scout for the Cincinnati Reds, and he was impressed with my performance. Enough so that he made a call to the Reds offices to tell them about this kid he saw pitching down in Tennessee.

CINCINNATI COMES A KNOCKIN'

I had a pretty good season at Wesleyan, but I still wasn't getting much attention from the scouts. I should have worried about my chances of getting signed then, but for some reason, I didn't. I just kept pitching and hoping for the best.

Toward the end of my senior year, we headed to David Lipscomb College for a conference tournament.

There was actually a chance we would have hosted the tournament at our place if we would have beaten the Railsplitters of Lincoln Memorial University earlier in the season. We were ahead 8-1 in the bottom of the ninth. I assured the coach I was fine to go on, but he pulled me—and Lincoln went on to score eight runs and beat us 9-8.

That's the way it goes sometimes.

Anyway, after one of our tournament games, I finally got some good news. Chet Montgomery, a Cincinnati scout who had been told about my performance against Kentucky earlier that spring, made the trip to the tournament and said he was there to watch me pitch. He asked if I'd be interested in coming to the Reds predraft tryout day at Riverfront Stadium after the college season.

Those tryouts were great opportunities to impress the clubs and get drafted, so, of course, I was interested. For as long as I wanted to be a pro ballplayer, I wanted to be a Cincinnati Red.

I couldn't believe that the only team showing any interest just happened to be the Reds, my favorite team.

LOOKING LIKE RONNIE

To get ready for my tryout, I needed a major makeover. I was as far from looking like a Cincinnati Red as possible.

Cincinnati ballplayers were required to be clean cut and shaven back then, and I had a big hippy mop of hair and a moustache.

Although I was only trying out, I went ahead and got a haircut and shaved my face clean. It was probably futile, but I didn't want the Reds to have any doubts about my ability to fit into their system. Plus, I knew the Reds might be my only shot at making it.

I decided I should model my new look after the poster boy for Cincinnati ballplayers: Ronnie Oester. No one could wear a uniform better than him. Everything always fit perfectly, from his perfectly placed stirrups up to the perfectly creased bill of his hat.

Even today, the Reds hang a picture of Ronnie in all of the minor league clubhouses so the young guys know how the uniform is supposed to be worn.

TRYING OUT

I made the drive to Cincinnati with Debbie, my girlfriend and future wife, from her mom's place in Florida.

It was a long ride. In fact, we were lucky to get there at all. We took her old Toyota Celica. On the way back home, the thing belched black smoke so rancid I had to cover my face with a T-shirt for most of the drive.

But none of that really mattered to me. I was focused only on the tryout.

I was anxious for most of the trip down. I wasn't really nervous, though—just excited to get there and show them what I could do.

Walking onto the field at Riverfront Stadium for the first time was amazing. I had never been in the stadium, let alone walked on the actual field that the Big Red Machine played on. As a lifelong Reds fan, it felt like holy land.

There were a lot of guys at the tryout, and I was one of the older ones at 22. I knew this was probably my last shot at making a case for playing in the bigs. No other teams had really shown any interest, and none had invited me to a tryout. It was Cincinnati or bust, as far as I was concerned.

Most of the tryout is now just a blur. For most of the afternoon, I just threw on the side. If they liked what they saw, they'd call your number and stick you on the mound to face real batters. At first I didn't hear them call my number, but Larry Doughty, the Reds assistant scouting director, assured me they did and said he'd try to squeeze me in at the end of the session. Time was running out, though, because the Reds players started coming onto the field to get ready for that night's game. And as happy as I would have been to try to snag an autograph or talk shop with those guys, I knew I was there for another reason.

Luckily, they got me on the mound just in time.

"Why don't you throw a few fastballs," Doughty said to me.

I threw a few.

"OK, how about some breaking balls?"

I threw some more. I felt good about my performance, and just like that, it was all over.

Doughty then came over to me.

"Where are you going to be on draft day? Just in case."

I told him, but I wasn't really expecting a call.

That was that. They saw what I had to offer, and the decision was theirs to make.

In return for my appearance, I got a ticket to the Reds game that night and didn't dwell on the tryout, because I was so into the game.

After the game, I headed back to Florida and hoped draft day would bring good news.

DRAFT DAY

On draft day, I waited by the phone down in Florida. I tried to play it cool and not think about it, but it was hard not to. There was no plan B for me, so my baseball future rested solely on the other end of that phone.

After some nervous pacing, it finally rang.

"Congratulations, Tom," Chet Montgomery said. "We just took you in the ninth round, 233rd overall. We've got some more calls to make, but a local scout will be giving you a call to work out the details."

That was it. I hung up the phone, and I couldn't have been happier. I was absolutely ecstatic. I thought it was strange that they were so cool about it.

Later that day, George Zuraw, a Florida scout, called just as Chet said he would. He said the team was offering a $3,500 bonus for me to sign.

"That sounds great," I said, "but do you think it is possible that I could get $5,000?"

"I'll call you right back," Zuraw said and hung up.

No sooner had I hung up the phone and relayed my counter-offer to Debbie did the phone ring again.

"They're gonna give you $3,500," he said bluntly. "Take it or leave it."

I said, of course, I would take it. But I still laugh when I think about the absurdity of them not budging on the extra $1,500.

George picked me up soon afterward and took me to the sporting-goods store, which I guess is a tradition after you get signed. He bought me a pair of cleats and a Wilson A2000 glove, which was just awful. I hated that thing. It didn't matter, though. I would have worn oven mitts to be a Cincinnati Red.

He gave me the option of reporting to Tampa or Billings, two of their Class A teams. My mom and stepfather had relocated to Billings not long before, so I opted for Montana.

And like that, I was a Cincinnati Red, albeit a minor leaguer. And the truth soon set in: The hard part was just beginning.

3

DOWN ON THE FARM

THE REDS WAY

It didn't take me long to realize that the Reds were a first-class organization from top to bottom. They expected nothing but the best from everyone within the system, and if you didn't follow suit, you were going to pay the consequences.

Things didn't start off well for the Billings team once we all arrived for the 1982 season. On the first night we were all officially under his control, Marc Bombard, our manager, busted 24 out of the 25 guys for breaking curfew. I was the only one left unscathed, and that was only because I was living at home, and they never bothered to check in on me.

Our punishment came in the form of an angry, screaming field coordinator named Mike Compton. *Field coordinator* was hardly a fitting title for him. *Drill sergeant* would have been more appropriate. He ran us into the ground, and he scared the living snot out of every one of us. We could barely walk when he was finished with us.

Coach Bombard then called us into the clubhouse for a meeting, where he, too, tore into us. He kicked a trashcan all over the clubhouse after doing a few laps around the place. He just lit into everyone, yelling and screaming.

Most of my teammates were 18- and 19-year-old kids who had probably never been away from home. They probably wondered if they had been sent to a baseball team or a prison. But I'm guessing most of them were superstars back in high school and after being drafted probably thought they were pretty hot stuff.

I was a little older and wiser. I knew the reasoning for the big production. It would be impossible to create a team atmosphere unless the egos and any sense of entitlement weren't checked at the door. We were the rawest of professional ballplayers. The odds of making it to the bigs were stacked against us. If we had any hopes of making it out of the minors, we were going to have do things their way.

I fell into line, kept my mouth shut, and just tried to learn everything I could.

MVP KALVOSKI

Joining me in Billings that year was Kalvoski "Kal" Daniels. He was a 1982 third-rounder of the New York Mets, but didn't sign with them and went to the Reds in the secondary phase of the draft.

I knew he was something special right away. Kal did everything that year. He hit about .370, led the league in stolen bases, showed off a great arm in the outfield, and ended up being the league's MVP. He was just an awesome player.

Kal ended up making the majors soon after I did, and he remained a great hitter. But he was cursed with two bad knees, and I think he took a lot of grief for being injured a lot. But I saw him when he was healthy and on top of his game, and he was about as good as they get.

You hear it said a lot, but with Kal, I know it's true: If he could have stayed healthy, he could have been one of the greatest players of our generation and certainly one of the best players ever to wear a Reds uniform.

SITUATIONS THAT STINK

I couldn't have asked for a better manager than Marc Bombard for my first season. Like me, "Bombie" used to be a left-handed pitcher, and like me, he wasn't exactly the biggest physical specimen.

I tried to learn as much as possible about pitching from him. He was a rookie manager in the Reds farm system that year, but he had the knowledge of a grizzled veteran.

Being a starting pitcher, I hated being pulled from a game, no matter how hard I was being hit. But Bombie taught me never to second-guess your skipper in those situations.

"When a manager comes out to get you, you don't ask any questions and you don't try to argue," he once told me. "You keep your mouth shut, and you gently place the ball in your skipper's hand like it's soft steamin' turd."

I understood his point, but the visual obviously left a little to be desired.

BOBBLEHEAD BOMBIE

Although Bombie was a great manager, he had no patience for losing.

I was pitching against the Helena Phillies in Montana that year against a guy named Rogers Cole. He beat me 1-0. When the game was over, the sun was still shining, because the game only took about an hour and a half. We had absolutely no offense, and I suffered the tough-luck loss. Bombie set a curfew for 11 p.m.

On the way back to the hotel, I picked up a couple Coors Light tallboys. I was 22, and the drinking age was 21. TBS replayed Braves games during the night, so I just wanted to relax and watch some baseball to take my mind off our game.

Bombie came in later that night to check curfew and saw the two empty beer bottles sitting on the table.

When Bombie got upset, he got really animated. He'd ask you a question over and over while his head bounced back and forth like one of those bobblehead dolls.

"What are those, Tom? What are those, huh? What are those?" he asked, pointing to the bottles and jerking his head back and forth like it was going to pop right off his neck.

Without trying to laugh, I explained that I thought it was okay since I was of legal age.

"What are the rules? What are the rules, Tom? Huh, what are the rules?" he asked, wiggling his head back and forth. "That'll be a $50 fine."

Fifty bucks?! Hell, I was only making $650 for the whole month. I didn't even know there was a rule about beer. I knew the younger guys weren't allowed to drink, but I assumed it was because they weren't old enough. I hadn't bought them anything anyway, just two beers for me.

The next day, Bombie called me into his office. I figured he was going to yell at me or fine me some more, but he apologized and said he knew it was tough to lose like that. He said he still had to fine me, though, but he was dropping it to $10.

I guess his emotions just got the best of him the night before. Like me, he just couldn't stand to lose.

GETTIN' THE GIST

I finished my season at Billings with a 4-8 record, but I had a respectable 3.89 ERA and led the league with 88 strikeouts in 88 innings pitched.

After the season, I was sent to the Fall Instructional League in Tampa. It was there that I met Rob Murphy, who became my roommate, a future major league teammate, and even the best man at my wedding.

"Murph" was a quick-witted guy. He was pretty laid back and into things like the outdoors and horses, so we had a lot in common. He also had a Porsche, and I needed a ride around town, so we became quick friends.

When we weren't trying to find the best happy hour hangouts on the Dale Mabry Highway in Tampa, Murph and I both worked hard with Harry Dorish, our pitching coach and a former major league reliever. He was a great coach, but at 62 years old, he just didn't understand our sense of humor. So we just concentrated on our work.

Harry eventually taught me a screwball, which I used as a change-up. That pitch revolutionized my ability to get hitters out, and it was a big reason for my eventual success in the bigs. I struggled with the pitch at first, but I was soon cruising. It seemed like I got out everyone with it.

Harry, obviously pleased with his quick learner, then shared with Murph and me his secret to success.

"Fellas," he said one day, "learn your three pitches and master them, and you'll be driving a Cadillac in no time."

Murph just couldn't help himself.

"But Harry," Murph quipped, "I already drive a Porsche."

Murph and I were cracking up, but Harry had a deadpan look on his face. He must have thought we were idiots.

"I don't think you get the gist of my meaning, son," he said, shaking his head while he walked away.

WHAT A BABE

The only minor league camp I ever attended was in 1983. Although I was some no-name kid, I made quite the impression with the veterans.

I was usually a pretty mellow guy. I was much more likely to sit back and observe everything going on than to seek out any type of attention. I just usually kept my mouth shut and did my work. But at camp, I got the opportunity to win over some of the older guys.

Back in college, Jimmy Deshaies used to do a great impersonation of Babe Ruth. His signature swing, the heavy-footed trot—the whole shebang. So he taught me how to do it, and I had it down pat. Besides, back then, I was built like a miniature version of the Babe, so I really looked the part.

Although I was over at the Redsland complex with the rest of the minor leaguers that spring, the major leaguers had heard of my famous impersonation and called me over to Al Lopez Field to put on a skit before one of their games.

They made it a whole pregame production. I stuffed a pillow into my jersey, took a few swings, connected on an imaginary home run, and trotted around the bases just like the Babe. The guys loved it, especially the veterans like Johnny Bench and Dave Concepcion.

When I got called up to the majors the following season, a few guys had remembered me—but not as Tom Browning. I was known simply as the Babe Ruth guy.

FLEEING THE SCENE

I began 1983 with the Tampa Tarpons in the Florida State League. With my new screwball, I plowed through the league, going 8-1 with a 1.49 ERA with 101 strikeouts in 78⅔ innings pitched. I then got a promotion to Class AA Waterbury.

I was making great strides in the system, and I just wanted to keep advancing.

Waterbury, though, was a bad team that struggled to score runs. However, I knew I just had to concentrate on my own pitching and things would work out.

One of my starts for the the Tarpons came in New Britain, Connecticut, but I missed the team bus, which is one of the dumbest mistakes you can make as a minor leaguer.

I begged, pleaded, and finally got my roommate to drive me to the ballpark. I knew I was in deep for missing the bus, especially since I was scheduled to pitch that day.

We were cruising along, and it looked like I was actually going to make it to the park in time. And then it happened. We were just a block or so from our destination, and bam! We got sideswiped by another car. We were both fine, but my roommate's truck was in pretty bad shape. But I still had to get to the ballpark, so I grabbed my stuff out of the back, told him I was sorry, and made a dash for it. I never did figure out how he got home.

Jim Lett, our manager, told me I was fined $25 for being late, but that I still would get the start. And if I was rattled from the crash, it didn't show on the mound. I threw an absolute gem that day—a complete-game one-hit shutout.

HITTING MY SPOTS

The key to my success was being able hit my spots consistently. A pitcher can have a 100-mile-per-hour fastball, but if he can't throw his pitch where he wants to, he's not going to make it very far.

As I progressed through the Reds farm system, that consistency became more and more important.

I could blow a 92-mile-per-hour fastball past a kid in Class A, but it took some craftiness to get the better players out at places like Waterbury.

It required more command and ability to adjust your game plan on the fly. When the count got into the hitter's favor, they didn't miss very often. But being able to adjust my speeds and place the ball where I wanted to made the job a lot easier.

4

THE BRINK OF THE BIGS

IN THE MACHINE'S SHADOWS

The city of Cincinnati has always embraced the Big Red Machine teams of the 1970s. I'm sure they always will. They even made a Reds fan out of me when I was a kid and living a couple thousand miles away.

When I entered camp in 1984 as a non-roster invitee, Tony Perez and Davey Concepcion were still with the major league club, and Johnny Bench was around as an instructor. They were three of the stars of the Big Red Machine, and everyone just swarmed to them. Not just fans, but other players and coaches and anyone associated with baseball. Everyone wanted to be around them.

I remember sitting on the bus a few times during spring that year and brazen fans would walk right onto the bus hoping to snag autographs from those Big Red Machine guys. I guess they just had that type of charm and appeal, even when their careers were winding down.

I knew how those fans felt, though. If I weren't in uniform and trying to earn a spot on the team, I probably would have been right there with them trying to grab an autograph of my own.

PARKER IN THE BUFF

Although free agency had been around since 1976, Dave Parker was the first real free agent the Reds ever signed.

After winning the MVP with the Pirates in 1978, his knees started getting banged up, and he soon fell out of favor with the Pittsburgh fans. The Reds took a gamble and picked him up prior to the 1984 season, which was great because I always admired the guy. He ended up being one of the funniest guys I met in baseball, too.

We had a pitchers' meeting the first day of camp that spring at the Redsland minor league complex in Tampa. We were sitting in the middle of the clubhouse to discuss what we'd all be doing to get ready for the season.

"Park," who had reported to camp early that year, came into the clubhouse to work out early and headed to his locker, which was right near our meeting.

Back then, he was one of baseball's superstars. Most of the guys in the meeting were younger, and I think we all kind of paused just to try to comprehend how cool it was that we were actually sharing a clubhouse with a guy like him. Naturally, we couldn't help glancing over at him.

Wondering what in the hell we were staring at, Dave asked, "What? Ain't you guys ever seen a black man naked before?"

SWEATING THE SMALL STUFF

I was at my first major league camp that year, and I was in pretty bad shape and a little chunky.

One of the things we did to work on our conditioning during camp was running poles, which meant that we ran from foul pole to foul pole across the outfield.

I was running with Bruce Berenyi, who resembled a charging rhino when he ran. He could run forever. I, on the other hand, was sucking wind, and my lungs felt like they were on fire. I just couldn't keep up with him, but I didn't want anyone to know, so I just pushed myself until I was completely and utterly exhausted.

Soon after, we all got together to stretch. This was still part of warmups, but I was already sweating pretty badly. Perspiration was never a problem for me. I could sweat in a snowstorm. But after running in 85-degree weather, I was soaked.

Vern Rapp, the Reds manager, walked by and saw me all sweaty. I probably looked a little nervous, too.

"Relax, rookie," he said. "It's only stretching. We're not going to cut you yet."

PARKER AT THE PLATE

During camp back then, pitchers threw batting practice. We were supposed to use that time to work on pitching from the stretch and from the windup, and basically just to get our legs back under us. Dave Parker pulled me aside early that spring with some advice.

"Listen, this is batting practice for us," he said. "You're not trying to throw your best pitches here. You're not trying to strike us out. Just work on your delivery and throwing the ball over the plate."

I understood. This was early camp, so everyone was a little rusty. It wasn't an audition, Park said. It was just a chance for everyone to get back into baseball mode.

Park was one of the first guys I faced after our talk. I threw a strike, and he crushed it for a home run. I threw another, and he crushed another one. And these weren't cheap home runs.

Apparently, Dave wasn't feeling too rusty.

After the third rocket cleared the right field wall and landed in the parking lot, he stepped out of the box with a little smile on his face.

"Did that one hit my Porsche?" he asked me. "Tell me it didn't hit my Porsche!"

I thought he was kind of rubbing it in, so I threw the next one right under his chin. After all, I was just doing what he told me to—there was no reason to rub it in.

Park just backed off and smiled after that pitch. He knew I said everything I needed to with just that one pitch.

I went back to throwing strikes, and he went right back to hitting home runs. But I never heard another damn thing about that car of his.

STAR STRUCK

In spring that year, George Brett was the first batter I faced from an opposing team.

One of my best friends growing up had scribbled "God" above a poster of George, and all I kept thinking was here I am, trying to strike out the Almighty. After working the count to 0-2, I thought I might just get him out. But then I threw a fastball inside that he smashed to the left field wall for a double.

Steve Balboni, another well-known slugger, then came up and crushed one off the center field wall for extra bases.

These were the first real major league opponents I had faced, and it wasn't looking good.

But I learned that the quicker you forget *whom* you are facing, the quicker you can work on actually getting them out. That was one of the biggest lessons I took away from camp that year.

I just started looking at them like they were any other player, and they started making outs like everyone else. Even the Lord, a.k.a. George.

WHAT A RELIEF

The other non-roster invitee I remember in camp that year was Mike Konderla, who was also drafted in 1982 and finished the previous season in high-A ball. But it didn't matter. Mike could have finished the year in tee-ball, and he still would have had the confidence that he belonged in the majors. You had to love guys like that.

Every night we'd go back to our headquarters at the Tampa Hilton, and Mike kept telling me he thought we both had a good shot of making the team. Although it's nice to set your sights high, I wasn't shooting for the moon.

I had finished 1983 in Class AA and just wanted to at least make it to Class AAA in 1984. Making the big league club would have been nice, but I knew I was making progress in the Reds system if I at least got to Class AAA, so that's what I concentrated on.

As camp neared an end, I found out that Vern Rapp wanted to bring me to Cincinnati with the big league club—but as a relief pitcher.

To be honest, the Reds stunk that year. They hadn't been good for a couple of years, and 1984 didn't look like it was shaping up to be much better. I wouldn't have minded bypassing Class AAA if it meant I would be in the starting rotation, but I wasn't too crazy about being a reliever.

Growing up, I remember the general notion that your starters were prospects and your relievers were suspects. I had never been a reliever, and I had no desire to be one.

Luckily, Bob Howsam had a plan for my future in the organization, and he stepped in and told Vern that he wanted me to stay a starter, so I was headed for Class AAA Wichita. Although I was disappointed I wouldn't be with the major league club out of camp, I found some comfort in knowing I'd be staying in a starting rotation.

FOR STARTERS...

You could say I wasn't very superstitious. Well, I wasn't superstitious four out of five days, anyway.

You see, knowing exactly when I was going to pitch and being able to prepare for it—physically and mentally—obviously played a big part in my success as a pitcher. The idea of becoming a reliever never appealed to me. I liked the routine of starting. I liked knowing exactly when I was slated to pitch so that I could focus all of my concentration and energy around that one day. I liked being the guy who could start a game and possibly finish it.

However, being a reliever required a completely different mindset. You had to be ready to pitch at any moment on any day. In the years that followed, I would see guys who excelled at it—John Franco and Rob Dibble, for example. But I just knew it wasn't for me.

That's why I wasn't too disappointed when they sent me to Class AAA. I knew I'd eventually get my shot, and thanks to Bob Howsam, it would likely be in the starting rotation.

TOUGH OUTS

It was in Class AAA that I learned what it took to get out major league hitters. Unlike the lower minor leagues, in Class AAA you play against major leaguers on their way down and guys on their way up, like Terry Pendleton and Vince Coleman.

Guys like that forced you to throw your pitches perfectly. You couldn't get away with bad pitches without getting punished. If you accidentally hung one over the plate, they were going to make you pay for it.

I suffered some growing pains, but my season at Class AAA turned out pretty well. I went 12-10 with a league-best 160 strikeouts, and I finished second in innings pitched.

I thought the big league club would have to notice me sooner or later.

PETE COMES HOME

In August that year, we were playing the Denver Bears in Colorado. That's when we heard the news than Vern Rapp had been fired as the Reds manager and replaced with Pete Rose, whom Bob Howsam acquired from Montreal to take over as the club's player/manager.

Talk about a breath of fresh air and an incentive to get promoted to the majors!

Everyone knew Pete was going to turn things around. All of the guys who had been sent down earlier in the year couldn't wait to get back. And all of the guys who were hoping to get called up would get the bonus of playing for Pete. Everyone wanted to get to Cincinnati that year.

I was just hoping I'd be one of them.

Earlier in the year, a lot of pitchers were getting promoted to the major league club, including John Franco, Ron Robinson, and Brad Lesley. But despite my solid year, I wasn't one of them. I was a little disappointed, but I didn't worry about it too much because a lot of things played into those types of decisions, such as the club's specific needs, player options, and all kinds of other stuff.

I understood the process and accepted it. I knew I'd eventually make it, but the thought of playing for Pete definitely made the waiting a little tougher.

CINCINNATI CELEBRATES

By 1984, a number of Reds fans were probably still bitter about the midseason strike three years earlier. Cincinnati didn't really field any competitive teams in the years that followed, so fan apathy seemed to really sink in. Despite being in the farm system, I was still a devoted fan myself, and seeing the major league club struggle was disappointing.

Once Pete was named manager and was back with the Reds where he belonged, I celebrated like all of Cincinnati did. We were sure he'd be the spark that was needed to get the club back on track.

I still remember hearing about his first game back in the lineup. Pete did it like only he could.

Batting second, he lined a first-inning pitch. The center fielder bobbled the ball, and Pete rounded second base and headed for third. In his trademark style, he belly-flopped headfirst into third base and was called safe.

They say the entire crowd, which delayed the start of the game by 10 minutes because of all the last-minute walkup sales, erupted into a thunderous roar as the Reds went on to win.

I would have paid anything to see it for myself, but I thought my chance would be coming soon enough.

A DIFFERENT SHADE OF RED

Jim Fregosi is probably best remembered as the guy who was traded to the New York Mets for Hall of Famer Nolan Ryan. However, he had a fine career of his own. He was an All-Star shortstop, and after his retirement, he immediately began a second career as a baseball manager.

One of Fregosi's early jobs was skipper of the Louisville Redbirds, which in 1984 was the Class AAA affiliate for the St. Louis Cardinals.

I was enjoying a solid season for Wichita that year and was apparently getting some attention from other teams.

I caught up with Jim at the baseball winter meetings in 2004, where he told me about a potential deal that could have completely changed the course of my career.

"Tom," he said, "you have no idea how close you were to becoming a Redbird and playing for me."

I was caught completely off guard. That was the first time I had ever heard about the trade. Apparently, the Cardinals had made a deal for me, but Bob Howsam said he wanted to watch one more of my starts before he pulled the trigger.

Luckily, that start turned out to be a masterpiece, one of the best games of my career. With future Reds manager Dave Miley as my catcher, I pitched my first professional no-hitter, a seven-inning gem in the first game of a doubleheader against the Iowa Cubs.

And, of course, the Reds never traded me.

MY DEFINING MOMENT

The morning after my no-hitter, I had breakfast with Chet Montgomery, the Reds scout who got me drafted. I didn't realize it at the time, but he was probably in town to tell me I had been traded. Luckily, my no-hitter kept that from happening.

Chet congratulated me on my ascent through the Reds farm system. He was pleased with my progress and probably feeling a bit proud that he was the one who had discovered me.

But I couldn't help but think back to two years earlier. On draft day, Chet had told me the Reds were willing to give me a $3,500 signing bonus. I had asked him for $5,000, and he had said they were offering the $3,500—take it or leave it. When I reminded Chet of the irony, he just smiled.

"Well, you're going to make your money in the big leagues anyway," he told me. "So I wouldn't worry about that."

Of all the events in my career, that was probably my one defining moment. As a young player, you think you have an idea of where you fit into the system, but you never know for sure. And I was scared to death of those front-office guys, so it's not like I was ever going to ask. But for the first time, I got assurance that I was in the Reds' plans and had a real future with the club.

JUST THAT LUCKY

From the very first day you get drafted, you're always told that your goal should be to get to the majors, but not necessarily with the club that drafted you. I have a weird memory, and certain phrases have always stuck in my craw. And that phrase was definitely one of them that I always thought about.

In our breakfast meeting, Chet had kind of alluded to the fact that I might be called up later that year. It almost seemed to good to be true. Could I really buck the odds and actually make it to the majors with the club that drafted me? The club that meant so much to me even as a kid?

It felt like a baseball fan's wildest dreams coming true. I just concentrated on my continued success at Class AAA and hoped for the best. I almost felt like I would jinx it if I thought about it too much. That's how much playing for the Cincinnati Reds meant to me.

BIG LEAGUE BOUND

After our final game of the season for Wichita, manager Gene Dusan told us a few guys were headed to the big league club for September callups. Dann Billardello, Wade Rowdon, Fred Toliver, and Alan Knicely would all be joining me on our way to Los Angeles for a Dodgers–Reds series.

Obviously, we were all thrilled. For me, it was a lifelong dream come true.

I flew into Los Angeles, checked into my hotel, and left early for the ballpark. New to the big leagues, I had to get directions to Dodger Stadium, then to the clubhouse, and then on how to actually get into the clubhouse. Rookies never know that kind of stuff.

Once I made it there, it was like walking into a dream. I can remember it as clearly as ever, strolling by the lockers of Dave Concepcion, Tony Perez, and Dave Parker, and seeing their jerseys hanging by mine. That's when I knew I had really made it. I was now sharing a clubhouse with my idols.

At the time, I had no idea how the Reds were planning to use me during that final month of the season, or if they were going to use me at all. I was just happy to be there.

Then, the first guy came up to introduce himself. It was none other than Pete Rose, the guy we all couldn't wait to play for.

"Welcome Tom," he said, offering me a handshake. "Welcome to the club."

I was so nervous, I didn't even know what to call him. Skip? Mr. Rose? I finally settled on, "Thanks, Pete."

"Oh, one quick thing," Pete added, "Mario Soto's wife went into labor. He had to go back home. You're starting on Sunday. Welcome to the bigs."

REDEMPTION FOR A DODGERS HATER

It was a Sunday day game, September 9, and I was scheduled to pitch my major league debut against the Dodgers. As a lifelong Reds fan, I naturally despised Dodger blue. They were bitter rivals in the 1980s. And here I was, pitching in the majors for the first time—against them—in their home park.

I was scared to death.

Like any big game in my career, it took me a while to find my legs. Do you know what it means when a ballplayer says that? They seriously can't feel their legs underneath them. You have so much adrenaline rushing through your body, you can't even figure out how you're standing upright. You're numb to everything.

I remember walking down to the bullpen to warm up and just trying to keep my nerves in order. I told myself to stay calm and collected, and treat it like any other start, but I couldn't even fool myself. I knew what a big deal it was, so I just tried to warm up like I usually did and forget about everything else.

We wore our practice jerseys with the red mesh that day. I'm not sure why we didn't wear our regular jerseys, but I would have worn my pajamas and a G-string if they told me to. I was nervous, but I had waited my whole life for that day.

The game finally started, and I was countering Dodgers rookie Orel Hershiser, who was having a fine year of his own.

I struck out my first batter, Dave Anderson, and gave up my first hit to Pedro Guerrero in the second inning. Guerrero kept stepping out on me the whole game. He probably didn't appreciate some Cincinnati rookie working so quickly and getting him out of his rhythm, so I ended up throwing one pitch right under his chin. I think he got the message, and I started feeling like I was in control.

The Reds ended up getting two runs in the fourth, and that was all I needed.

I cruised into the ninth inning with a shutout before giving up three straight hits. Teddy Power came in to get the last two outs, and we won 5-1.

I pitched pretty well—11 hits over 8⅓ innings with one run, two walks, and four strikeouts. I also got the win.

All in all, it was a great day. And most importantly, I couldn't have picked a better opponent for it to come against.

GUARD DOG

It didn't take me long to see how the veterans kept everyone in check.

After my successful debut, I was being interviewed by some of the media. I was on cloud nine, oblivious to anything going on around me, including our departing bus.

Tony Perez, the main veteran of the club, gave me a warning.

"Hey rook, you pitched a great game," he said, "but that doesn't mean we won't leave you here. Get on the bus. Now."

One of the umpires was generous enough to give me the Dodgers' lineup card from my major league debut on September 9, 1984. *Photo courtesy of Tom Browning*

I'm sure a lot of the other guys wanted to say the same thing to me, but "Doggie" (a nickname Pete gave him) took it upon himself. As the club's elder statesman, he wanted to make sure all the greenhorns knew someone was looking over their shoulders.

DEB'S DELIVERY

I was lucky to have gotten the opportunity to start a game after my September callup. I figured I'd be lucky just to get a couple relief appearances that month.

Mario Soto was pretty well entrenched in the starting rotation at the time. After all, the guy had struck out 500 batters in the previous two seasons, so I knew they weren't going to bump someone like him from the rotation to make room for a kid like me. Luckily, though, the birth of his daughter came at the perfect time.

However, when my wife was ready to give the birth to our daughter, I knew I didn't have the job security Mario did. After my successful debut, Pete gave me another start, and I pitched well in a no-decision against the Padres.

But even after those two starts, I wasn't sure if I'd get another one.

Late on Thursday night, September 20, 1984, Debbie called and said the baby would be arriving soon. I called Pete and said I was flying out the next morning, but that I would definitely be back in time for the game.

I flew back home to Wichita early that Friday morning, but missed the birth of my daughter, Tiffany, by an hour. Once I got there, I spent some time just staring at her and talking to Deb. It was great spending the day with them, but I was due back in Houston the next day for a 7:35 p.m. start against the Astros.

I made it back and went straight to the ballpark. I think Pete thought I was nuts when I told him I was absolutely ready to pitch that night. He probably thought baseball was the last thing on my mind, but I knew I needed to close out the season in impressive fashion.

PINCH-HITTING PETE

After two solid outings, I wanted to finish the year on a strong note and make a case for a spot in the rotation for the following year.

A sparse crowd entered the Astrodome and settled in for what would become a real pitchers duel.

I was just making my break into the big leagues when my daughter, Tiffany, was born. A few years later she and Debbie joined me at Riverfront Stadium during Family Day.
Photo courtesy of the Cincinnati Reds

I was shutting down the Astros, but Mike Scott was doing the same to our lineup. I had scattered a few hits and a run over seven innings, but the game was tied 1-1. In the top of the eighth, Brad Gulden led off the inning and drew a walk. Pete, who didn't start that day, put in Gary Redus to pinch run.

I was due to bat, and I was getting ready to grab some lumber when Pete stopped me.

"I'm going to hit for you."

"I'm fine," I said.

I was feeling good and could pitch a few more innings. I didn't need a pinch hitter. Besides, I really wanted to get the win.

"No, *I* am going to hit for you," Pete repeated.

"Oh," I said, almost apologetically, as I headed straight for the bench.

As far as I was concerned, you didn't question a guy with 4,000 career hits.

(For the record, Pete struck out.)

CASPER FLASHBACK

The day after the last game of the season, I went to the clubhouse to gather my belongings before I headed home for the winter.

I was happy to see Pete there. He was in his boxers and watching TV, which wasn't all that unusual. The clubhouse was really like his second home back then.

Pete looked a little pensive, and he told me he was just hanging out there for a while before heading to the hospital. Carol was being prepped to give birth to his son, Tyler, and he was just trying to stay busy to keep his mind off of things until he left. I had experienced the same excitement and anxiety of being an expectant father just a few weeks prior, so I wanted to help provide a distraction.

"Guess what, Pete?" I said. "You're actually older than my mom. Can you believe that?"

It was great just joking around with him like that for a while. I couldn't have asked for a better ending to my season—getting to spend some time with my hero and manager. We didn't even really talk much about the season, just personal stuff about our lives and families and plans for the winter.

I told Pete about the trip he made to our Little League banquet in Casper back when I was a kid and how much it meant to me. Pete smiled and said he remembered the night well. He said he still had the cowboy hat that we had given him as a gift.

Our brief conversation was one of the highlights of my year. If you had told me back in camp that I'd be hanging out with Pete Rose in a Riverfront Stadium clubhouse in six months, I probably would have laughed at you. But there I was, enjoying an hour of my life I'll never forget.

BIG LEAGUES, BIG BUCKS

I'm a simple guy with simple tastes. Old jeans, some beatup cowboy boots, cheap beer, country music, and a Chevy Blazer were about all I ever bought or needed.

However, once I got to the major leagues, it was hard not to notice the big bucks that came with the job. In 1982 I was drafted by the Reds with a signing bonus of $3,500. I was making just $650 per month in rookie ball that year and got a raise to $700 per month once I got to Tampa. It bumped to $750 at Class AA and a hefty $1,500 when I got to Class AAA.

In the majors, though, is where the pay scale really started to increase. After my September callup, I earned a check for about $2,400 for two weeks' work. Two weeks!

The next year, veteran catcher Bo Diaz leaned over and said, "Hey, rook, look at this."

He showed me a check for $80,000. I'm assuming he earned that same check every two weeks, and it wasn't exactly pocket change. And he was hardly the highest-paid guy on the team.

I never did get used to the money. It's hard to believe we made so much for doing something I would have done for free.

WINTER CONDITIONING

After the 1984 season, I headed back to Utah, with my wife and daughter, to live with my mom and stepfather, who had relocated there the previous year.

I spent most of that winter counting down the days until February. I knew I had a pretty good shot of making the team out of camp, and I couldn't wait to get started.

My goal that winter was to get in shape. I took a job at a health club and ran 30 minutes on the treadmill before I opened the place and another 30 minutes before I left at night. I must have dropped 10 percent of my body fat during those months. I was fitting into pants I hadn't worn in years. But most importantly, I was getting myself in great shape for what I was hoping would be my first full season in the majors.

While working at the health club, I ended up meeting Dane Iorg, an outfielder/first baseman for the Kansas City Royals. Dane was good friends with Jim Kaat, the Reds pitching coach. Kaat told Dane that I had a good shot at making the team. Knowing that, Dane kept me motivated that offseason, even getting me to play racquetball with him a few times.

I ended up making a good friend in Dane. He told me about some of the smaller things about life in the bigs. Plus, it was just good to be around someone so competitive.

I also got my first and only agent that winter, a guy who represented Bill Landrum, one of my teammates in the minors. John Stupor got me a deal with Converse, who supplied me with the greatest cleats ever made. And Rawlings also signed me to a deal.

For the most part, I had done everything I could think of to get ready for the upcoming season, and I just wanted camp to start.

5

ROOKIE SUCCESS

IT'S IN THE NUMBERS

Want to know the odds of making a major league team out of spring training?

It's all in the numbers. Or to be more specific, the uniform numbers. The smaller the number, the better your chances of making the team. Anything higher than 50, and you've probably got reason to worry.

I wore No. 54 in camp in 1984. I had a good spring and made their decision to send me down a tough one, but I was eventually shipped to Class AAA. Besides, as a non-roster invitee wearing a number like that, I knew that their minds were probably made up before I even got to camp.

But in the spring of 1985, I knew my chances of making the club were pretty good. I had had a solid season at Class AAA Wichita in 1984, and my September callup had been an unquestionable success.

Once I got to camp that year, my prediction seemed likely. I walked into the clubhouse and saw a beautiful sight. Stitched on my uniform was a lovely 32.

FOUR SEASONS OF OPENING DAY

I don't remember Pete ever saying I made the club out of spring training, but I did, and I was thrilled. I couldn't wait for the season opener.

I've never been able to describe Cincinnati's Opening Day festivities to an outsider and do it justice. No city does it better. Cincinnati goes absolutely bonkers.

In 1985, I experienced my first one.

I think we saw all four seasons that day. It rained, and then the sun would come out, and then it would snow, and then the sun would come out, and then it would rain and snow again. It was like that all day, but it was obvious the packed house would have braved a lot worse conditions to be part of it. The crowd was awesome that day. There's nothing like the sound of thuds you get from 53,000 pairs of gloves and mittens clapping for your team.

Mario Soto started for us and pitched beautifully that day. Pete made the start at first and had a hand in every run we scored in the 4-1 victory over the Expos.

It was great just soaking in the whole atmosphere, but I knew I didn't want to be in the dugout for future openers. I wanted to be on the mound. And I guess the hope of maybe being an Opening Day starter was always in the back of my mind. As a Cincinnati pitcher and Reds fan myself, I couldn't think of a greater honor, especially after I witnessed Opening Day. That day just made me want the honor even more.

CALL ME PUGGY

Pete Rose had a nickname for everyone. Next to hitting, it was one of his best talents.

Within seconds of taking his first look at you, he'd give you a nickname that always stuck. Pete christened Ron "The True Creature" Robinson, Chris "Spuds McKenzie" Sabo, and Rolando "Boom Boom" Roomes, among others.

I got tagged with the nickname "Puggy." Pete thought I looked like one of those smooshed-faced Pug dogs every time I reared up to throw a pitch, so he thought the name made perfect sense. It caught on pretty quickly and has stuck ever since.

Frankly, I was just happy that Dave Parker's suggested nickname didn't catch on. Otherwise, I would have been known as "Couch-Cushion Face" during my years in the bigs.

STARR OF THE GAME

I've seen some blowups in my day, some real first-class eruptions that led to ejections. But the most unlikely of all came on the first day of May in 1985.

We were playing the Braves at Riverfront, which still had the old artificial turf. The stuff was so worn down and faded, you couldn't even really see any contrast between the ball and the turf. It was just a horrible playing surface.

The weather was nasty that day, and only a few thousand people showed up for the game. By the fourth inning, we were getting clobbered, and the rain was relentless. Tom Hume came in to pitch, and every time he would try to plant his front foot after a pitch, he would slide into the splits toward home plate. That was a surefire way to get injured.

I remember Dave Parker hitting a bullet between home and first base, and the ball just hydroplaned all the way to the outfield wall. It first hit 40 feet from home plate and then didn't land again until it short-hopped the outfield wall. Poor Claudell Washington was playing right field and looked like he was on ice skates trying to get to the ball. No one could get any footing.

In the top of the fifth, the umps finally called for a rain delay, and it looked like the game might be over. But after about two and a half hours, they called us back on to the field.

The field hadn't improved any, though. Larry Starr, the Reds trainer, pointed out the stupidity of playing in the conditions and argued that someone was really going to get hurt. Home-plate umpire Bruce Froemming, usually one of the league's better umps, said they were going to finish the game come hell or high water.

That set Larry off. He couldn't believe someone was stupid enough to allow us to keep playing. I respected Larry for standing his ground and looking out for the guys on the field, but Bruce didn't agree. He gave Larry the boot.

I remember asking someone on the bench, "Can you even eject a trainer? Is that allowed?"

I guess so. Larry was definitely tossed and sent to the clubhouse.

After five innings, they could have called the game and it would have counted as official. And because the score was so lopsided, I don't think anyone would have really objected.

But I think Larry had ticked off Bruce so much, he refused to call the game early. So we had to sit through a full nine innings of misery. Larry, though, stayed nice and toasty with his seat in the clubhouse.

BO KNOWS

The catcher who did the most for my young career was Bo Diaz.

The friendly Venezuelan was a 10-year veteran catcher to such legends as Steve Carlton, Bert Blyleven, and Jerry Koosman. I used to love to pick his brain about those guys, and in the process, he helped me become a better pitcher. He taught me all of the little things a pitcher needed to get a hitter out, how to handle runners on base, and how a little craftiness can get you out of just about any jam.

When his pitchers failed, he often took responsibility. When we succeeded, though, Bo gave us all the credit. He was a quiet leader, but he commanded our respect.

During my rookie season, Bo caught me often. I remember a few times where he'd flash a sign, I'd shake him off, he'd flash the sign again, and I'd shake him off again. He'd pause, and then calmly point to his head, letting me know he probably knew something that I didn't.

Who was I to question his judgment? Bo knew his stuff, and I trusted him completely.

In the spring of 1989, Bo learned the devastating news that his five-year-old son, Joshua, had been diagnosed with a brain tumor. He found it difficult to concentrate, and early in the season, he left the club and returned home to be with his family. Luckily, his son's health improved, and he was soon eyeing a comeback to the major leagues.

Unfortunately, I received word shortly after we won the 1990 World Series that Bo had been killed when the satellite dish he had been adjusting on the roof of his home fell on him. The tragic news hit the team, and me, awfully hard. Baseball had lost someone really special.

To this day, I remain thankful that I got to know Bo. He was a great teacher and a wonderful friend, and he helped me develop the confidence I needed to be a successful pitcher.

THAT'S MARGE

A few months into the 1985 season, I read in the papers that Marge Schott, the Reds' eccentric owner, was canceling the fireworks that they shoot off after each Reds' home run and win. She said they were too expensive, and she ended up taking a beating in the media because of it.

Luckily, we never really saw that side of Marge in the clubhouse. She really thought of all of us as her kids.

But Marge always made sure we had what we needed. Jim Ferguson, our publicity director at the time, used to tell us some horror stories about working in the front office with Marge—turning off computers that were left unattended to save electricity, checking the garbage to see if people were wasting paper, selling day-old doughnuts to employees. But we really didn't see that side of her.

If Pete needed a pitcher, Marge would go out and get us a pitcher. If she had to open her pocketbook to re-sign someone, she usually did it. She also kept ticket prices and concessions inexpensive for the fans, which made Riverfront a real fan-friendly place.

I don't think many people also knew how much she cared about winning. Although she'd let her emotions sometimes take over her decision-making, she always wanted a winning club. And it wasn't just for her. She felt like the city deserved a championship team.

As a ballplayer, you couldn't ask for more from an owner.

A GIANT HEADHUNTER

In 621 career at-bats, I hit just one triple. But I remember it well, more so than Mike Krukow, the pitcher who gave it up.

We were playing the Giants at Riverfront in June 1985, and I led off the third inning. I hit a shot to right-center field. Somehow, Dan Gladden and Chili Davis tripped over each other in the outfield. The ball wasn't even hit hard enough to get to the wall, but I was credited with a triple, and I was feeling pretty good about myself. We ended up scoring three runs that inning, and I had a nice lead.

I came up to bat the next inning, and Ronnie Oester was on third. I had a little swagger in my step as I came up to the plate, still proud of my first triple from the inning before. Now, I wanted to knock in Ronnie for my first career RBI.

Krukow, though, didn't seem to appreciate my hitting prowess or my newfound confidence. As I got settled in the batter's box, he stepped off the rubber and walked straight to home plate. He stared right at me and then looked at Bob Brenly, his catcher, with a determined look on his face.

"Don't worry, Bobby," the six-and-a-half footer said matter-of-factly. "If he squares around to bunt, I'll just throw it at his head."

It's amazing how the threat of a bean ball to the melon can affect your confidence in a situation like that. Now, no one was dumb enough to mistake Krukow for a standup comedian, and I had no idea how serious he was about splitting my head open. But the look on his face wasn't very reassuring.

I entered the box again, this time kind of gingerly. I was too nervous to even dig in with my spikes. Krukow knew he was in my head, and I was praying I'd just make it out of the at-bat with all of my body parts intact.

I took a few pitches before hitting a squibbler back to the pitcher's mound, and Krukow threw home in time to nail Ronnie.

Years later, I caught up with Krukow at some event and told him about the story. He just laughed. Apparently, I wasn't the first rookie he screwed with.

"I don't remember it," Krukow said with a huge smile on his face. "But I don't doubt it for a minute."

MR. RBI

All of our guys looked up to Tony Perez, especially the young hitters. Even Pete seemed to be in awe of the guy. He said of all the great hitters on the Big Red Machine, no one could come up with the big hits like Tony could. He was just the consummate RBI guy, even in 1985, when his career was coming to an end.

During a July game at Veterans Stadium, we were down a run in the top of the eighth. Dave Parker led off the inning with a triple, and Tony was up to bat.

I was sitting on the bench next to Pete, and he just looked at me and grinned.

"Watch this, Puggy," he said. "Right-center field. That's where it's going."

It wasn't so much a prediction as a statement of fact. It didn't sound like there was a single bit of doubt in his voice.

Sure enough, Tony laced a shot between center and right for a single. Park came around to tie the game, and we ended up winning it in extra innings.

TYING TY

One of the biggest news stories of 1985 was Pete's march toward hit No. 4,192. Everyone had been anticipating it since he returned to Cincinnati the year before, including all of the Reds' starting pitchers. We all wanted to be on the mound the day the record fell.

On September 8, Pete was two hits away from tying Ty Cobb's mark. However, he planned to sit out against Steve Trout, who was a left-hander. Pete hadn't started against a southpaw all season. But we found out that Trout had injured his elbow the night before after (of all things) he fell off a bicycle, so he was scratched from the game.

Right-hander Steve Patterson got the start instead, and Pete was back in the lineup.

Jay Tibbs started the game for us, and I just kept my fingers crossed that Pete could hold off for the record-breaker until my turn in the rotation.

He got No. 4,190 with a first-inning single, and then 4,191 in the fifth with another single. Pete had tied a record that many people thought could never be broken, and the crowd at Wrigley gave him a five-minute standing ovation for his efforts. It was a great show of class from the city, and they cheered like it was one of their own.

Pete got two more at-bats that day, and the crowd was roaring during each at-bat. But he grounded out in the seventh, and after a two-hour rain delay, struck out in the ninth. The game was eventually called because of darkness after nine innings as a 5-5 tie (Wrigley didn't have lights back then).

I wasn't too upset. I knew Pete would eventually get the hit, but I didn't want to be on the bench when it happened.

4,192

After tying Cobb's record, Pete didn't play the following day and went hitless in four at-bats on September 10. Luckily, on September 11, I was slated to pitch, and so was right-hander Eric Show for San Diego. So Pete put himself in the lineup.

Riverfront was packed, and all of the fans had one thing on their minds: 4,192.

I pitched a one-two-three inning in the top of the first, and after Eddie Milner made an out, Rose came up to bat in the bottom of the inning. The place was on its feet, and you could hear the cheers echo throughout the stadium. Although my big league career was only a year old, I had never heard something so loud. On a 2-1 count, Rose laced a shot to left-center field, which bounced in front of Carmelo Martinez for a hit.

The place erupted in celebration. The game must have been delayed for a good 40 minutes while they had an on-field ceremony. Pete was showered with applause and gifts. He even got a brand new Corvette from Marge with the license plate "PR 4192." She was like a proud mom that night and really made it a first-class event.

It was great being a part of the game, but as a pitcher, I was a little worried about the delay. I still had to pitch, and I could feel my arm getting cold.

Luckily, though, the delay didn't do much harm. I started right where I left off and ended up taking a shutout into the ninth. With two outs to go, though, Pete pulled me from the game. John Franco and Teddy Power closed it out to secure the victory.

For me, I knew I was part of history that night. And I know that no one will ever come close to breaking that record again.

After the game, I pleaded with Teddy to give me the ball from the last out.

"C'mon, I just want a memento from my win," I said, hoping he'd buy my b.s. excuse for wanting it.

But there was no way he was giving up that piece of memorabilia.

MY BUDDY

Buddy Bell was the epitome of a professional ballplayer.

He was traded to Cincinnati from the Rangers during the middle of the 1985 season, and he soon became one of my favorite veterans.

I remember watching Buddy during batting practice—not just hitting balls, but also taking grounders, throwing to first and second, working on every skill that he could need for the day's game. Like Tony Gwynn, he was the type of guy who worked on everything every day to stay sharp. To me, that's what a professional was: a guy who stayed on top of his game by concentrating on his strengths *and* his weaknesses.

In the minors, you're forced to be a selfish player. It's cutthroat down there. You're battling all of your teammates for a few coveted spots on the major league roster. Everyone has the same goal of making the big leagues, even though you know that just a handful will.

Luckily, once you do make it to the majors, the learning curve instantly takes off because you have guys like Buddy to learn from.

Buddy also taught me that downswings are inevitable. He struggled pretty badly when he first came over to Cincinnati, and the hits were few and far between.

We were playing the Braves late in the season, and it looked like Buddy was going to bust out of his slump when he laced a shot down the line. But the ball hit just a few inches foul, and I think he ended up striking out later in the at-bat.

We were at the Anchor Bar in Atlanta that night enjoying a few beverages and trying to console Buddy. He had a few vodkas in him, but he wasn't feeling sorry for himself.

"It's OK, guys. It's OK," he said. "I didn't need that hit anyway. I didn't need—"

And then, bam! He flipped right over his barstool and hit the ground.

The poor bastard just couldn't catch a break.

SLEEPING DODGERS

From a completely personal and selfish standpoint, I was obviously pleased with my performance in the second half of the 1985 season. I had every intention of staying in the Reds rotation in the following years, and I knew a solid rookie season would be a great first step toward that goal.

At the All-Star break, I was a respectable 7-7. But they made the decision to let me go ahead and start pitching on three days' rest in the second half, which I loved. I obviously wanted to log as many innings as possible, and pitching on three days' rest got me a few more starts each month.

On August 9, I dropped a tough one to Bob Welch and the Dodgers, and my record dropped to 9-9. But it turned out to be the last loss I notched the rest of the year.

After that start, I rattled off 11 straight wins to close out the season. I pitched really well, but like any good streak, I also experienced a good deal of luck.

One example was on September 15. We were hosting the Dodgers, and Dave Parker was still steaming about an argument he had had with

Dodgers catcher Mike Scioscia the day before. I told Park not to worry about it because I'd take care of things.

Talk about waking a sleeping giant. I plunked Scioscia in the top of the second, but it opened the floodgates. I got pounded that inning and gave up a ton of hits and three runs, and then they tagged me for three more runs a couple innings later. I figured my streak of consecutive wins was over, especially since Fernando Valenzuela was pitching lights-out for L.A. and had a 6-1 lead.

But the guys came through for me big time, scoring nine runs and chasing Valenzuela out of the game in the bottom of the sixth. The barrage of runs got me my 17th win of the season, although I seemed to do anything but deserve it.

I ended up winning my 20th game a couple weeks later.

In the years that followed, I learned that I was the first rookie to win 20 games since Bob Grim went 20-6 with the Yankees in 1954, and I was the first National Leaguer to do it since Harvey Haddix went 20-9 with the Cardinals in 1953.

Ironically, though, not one of us ever won 20 games in a season again.

KAAT HAPPY

When Pete was hired to manage the club at the end of 1984 season, he made good on a promise to his former Philly teammate and hired Jim Kaat as his pitching coach.

The hiring coincided well with my callup to the majors. "Kitty" was there for my three starts in 1984, as well as my official rookie year in 1985.

You could say that we were both cut from the same cloth. We both were left-handers, and we both liked to work quickly. Kitty, though, definitely had a little more success in his career, including 283 lifetime wins and 16 straight Gold Gloves.

"I won the first one on merit—and the 15 others on reputation," he used to joke.

I used to pick his brain about everything. He was a wealth of information. A kind of living timeline of baseball history, he was one of the few guys whose career spanned four different decades.

One of my favorite topics was Mickey Mantle. My dad was a big Mantle fan, and Kitty used to tell me about his amazing power. One time he threw The Mick a big looping curveball, and Mantle dipped down and crushed it out of the park—from one knee. Imagine the power that something like that would take.

He had a million stories like that.

Unfortunately, Kitty's coaching career was short lived. He left the Reds after the 1985 season so he could concentrate on broadcasting. I was obviously disappointed. I was hoping he'd be around for more than just that one year.

But he always tells me the same thing, "At least I can say I had a 20-game winner every year I coached."

NO QUIT IN RONNIE

I learned a lot about playing the game the right way during my rookie year, and one of the best lessons came during the last series of the year.

We were finishing the season on a West Coast trip, and Ronnie Oester was batting exactly .300.

Ronnie didn't wear batting gloves, so he used to develop blisters on his hands—really deep ones that would turn into full-fledged holes in his palms by the end of the season.

We were out of the playoff picture, and Ronnie had busted his hump all year, so Pete told him he had no problem sitting him if he wanted to stay at .300 for the year.

"Are you kidding?" he asked Pete. "That doesn't mean anything to me. I just want to win some games."

That's what I liked about Ronnie. He was just a great teammate. He didn't have a selfish bone in his body.

He ended up playing the remaining games and didn't hit much of anything. His average dropped to .295 for the season, but I doubt he even noticed.

COVER BOY

I was battling nerves my entire rookie season. I guess it was just the stress of playing in the bigs and the pressure of wanting to do well.

And I got shankers. Really bad ones. They're like cold sores you get during stressful times. I've gotten them a few times since then, but never like I did that first season in the majors. I was breaking out all the time.

Because of my slow start and plenty of other worthy stories to cover elsewhere in baseball, the media just didn't really notice me at first. That was fine, though, because I didn't need any more stress.

But after I put together two solid months to finish the season, *Baseball Digest* decided to do a cover story on me after the season. It touted me as an "Unheralded 20-Game Winner" and had some nice photos.

But if you look close enough at the pictures, you can see one of those damn shankers on my lip.

ROLLAWAY FAVORITE

Despite winning 20 games and pitching 260 innings, I was the runnerup in the NL Rookie of the Year voting. Vince Coleman, who stole a gazillion bases for the pennant-winning Cardinals, was the runaway favorite for the award and got every first-place vote.

But Vince never made it to the World Series. While he was warming up before an NLCS game, he got trapped by Busch Stadium's automated tarp as it unrolled across the infield. I remember seeing pictures of him being taken off the field in a stretcher. It was one of the most bizarre baseball injuries I had ever heard of.

I wasn't too bummed out about losing the award, though. Vince had a great year, and he was in the news all season. And although I had a great year of my own, I didn't really catch fire until late in the season, which was too late to garner much attention.

The Sporting News did name me the NL Rookie Pitcher of the Year that season, which was a nice honor. They gave me a big trophy, and I joined an impressive list of former winners, including Fernando Valenzuela, Dwight Gooden, and my good friend Bill Gullickson.

And as I'm sure you know, Vince bounced back just fine the following year, stealing another gazillion bases in 1986.

LET'S MAKE A DEAL

During my rookie year, I drove a Chevy Chevette, a hatchback piece of crap that rattled like it could explode at any moment.

As I was pulling into the stadium one day, Pete pulled up next to me in his Porsche. He took one look at my ride, heard the incessant rattling, and just shook his head.

I accept the *The Sporting News*'s Rookie Pitcher of the Year Award early in the 1986 season.
Photo courtesy of the Cincinnati Reds

He called me into his office later that afternoon and asked what in the hell I was driving. I told him I was still a rookie and not making a lot of money, so I hadn't looked for anything newer. Pete suggested I look around to see if a local dealership could work out a deal.

During our next road trip, my wife went over to Bob Noll's Suburban Chevrolet in Florence, Kentucky, and spoke to Bob about leasing car. He got my wife in a Chevy Celebrity, a nice family car and a suitable upgrade from my Chevette. Once he found out she was married to a Cincinnati Red, Bob told Debbie that I should come in and see him when I was back in town, so we could work out a deal for the payments. Apparently, he was a pretty big Reds fan.

I saw Bob a few days later, and he told me that he'd knock off a month's payment for every win I got the rest of the season. It was the end of June, and I was 4-4.

Poor Bob could have never expected the second half that I had. When all was said and done, I had won 20 games, and Bob was making my Chevy payments for the next year and a half.

MARGE SCORNED

After my 20-win season, Bob Noll asked Bengals quarterback Kenny Anderson and me about doing some commercials for his dealership. We both happily accepted the offer.

We filmed some radio spots and a few TV commercials, which were going to air that winter.

Soon after, the Reds had a year-end banquet, where I was honored as the Johnny Vander Meer Award recipient as the team's top pitcher that season.

Marge, though, was livid at the banquet and told Pete she was going to trade me. Apparently, Marge had a Chevrolet dealership of her own, which was news to me. I knew about the Buick dealership, but I no idea she had a Chevy dealership, too. Marge had heard about the spots I did for Bob, and she thought I was trying to show her up.

It made front-page news in Cincinnati, and a lot of people thought I might actually be shipped out of town.

But I apologized profusely to Marge and told her it was just a mistake. She eventually gave me a hug and told me not to worry about it.

They ended up pulling the TV ads before they ever aired, and I was back in Marge's good graces.

But no one in the clubhouse ever dared think about doing an ad for one of her rivals ever again. Not even 20 wins would give you that kind of freedom.

A KNIGHT IN BLOOMINGTON

Back in my playing days, many guys stuck around the city during the offseason. So Jim Ferguson, our publicity director, put together a field trip for us to go watch his former college buddy Bobby Knight coach Indiana University's basketball team at Assembly Hall.

I think Ronnie Oester, Buddy Bell, and Joe Nuxhall all made the trip with us, so I was in pretty good company.

We met Bobby in the hallway before the game, and the guy just scared the crap out of me. He was so tall and intimidating, he literally had me sweating—not that it took me much to sweat, of course. So I just kept my mouth shut and hoped he didn't notice.

I learned that night that different people lead in different ways, and there isn't just one successful way to go about it. Pete was a pretty intense manager, but Bobby took it to a whole new level. He roamed the sidelines like he was ready to pounce on someone at any moment. And he didn't react well to his players making stupid mistakes. He was so ticked at his team's effort in the first half, he locked them out of the locker room at halftime.

I don't think Bobby came back on the court until a few minutes after the second half started. But he seemed to get his message across because the Hoosiers came back and won the game.

Afterward, Bobby met us all for dinner. He was a huge baseball fan, so the conversation focused on the Reds and the upcoming season.

Besides, I don't think anyone was brave enough to ask him about the game or the halftime outburst.

6

CHARLIE HUSTLE AT THE HELM

CUSSIN' KURT

Kurt Stillwell was the Reds' first-round pick in 1983. He was such a promising prospect that they even considered moving Barry Larkin to second base in the minors just so they could keep Kurt on track at short.

In 1986, Kurt was hoping to head north with the rest of the major league club. Now, Kurt was a nice guy. Really nice. He was exceptionally polite and never cussed. Not once. I swear I don't think I heard him ever utter a single profanity, which is pretty rare among ballplayers.

As spring camp winded down, Pete called Kurt into his office to tell him the good news: He'd be heading to Cincinnati that year.

"But first," Pete said, "I wanna hear you say, 'F---!' Just once."

Kurt was probably just happy that he made the club, so he didn't really think much about the strange request.

"Umm, OK. F---!" he proudly said.

"Great, now you're coming north."

And that was that. Kurt was on the big league roster.

But I don't think Kurt made the club just because he said the f-word. Because if that were the only requirement, Pete would have had plenty of guys lining up to cuss him out.

LET IT RAIN

One of the best parts of having Pete as a manager was the occasional rain delay. He was a great storyteller, and during rain delays, we'd all get together in the clubhouse to hear about the pennants and World Series they won back in the 1970s.

For the younger guys, there was no bigger thrill.

Davey and Doggie were still on the team at that time, and they acted as Pete's supporting cast. Talk about living history.

It was just great remembering all of the events I watched as a kid and hearing it from their perspectives. Those memories, especially the ones from 1975 and 1976, were (and still are) rooted in me so deeply.

"There we are, in Game 7 of the 1975 World Series," Pete would say. "Thousands of people in Fenway Park are screaming. It's nut-crunch time. We're playing in the greatest World Series every played. And I look Carlton Fisk dead in the eye and ask, 'Is this a great game or what?'"

I must have heard about that Series a hundred times, and each time was better than the last. I never got tired of listening.

You could sense the intensity in Pete's voice every time. He just couldn't do anything half-assed, not even when it came to telling a story.

MULEPOWER

Dave Parker had some of the best one-liners, and Davey Concepcion was a target more than a few times.

One day Park was making fun of Davey's car. It was a Porsche, but Park argued that Davey's model had no horsepower and was probably powered by a mule. A few guys who overheard the conversation started laughing. Someone then walked by and asked what was so funny.

"Nothing really," Park said. "Davey was just telling me about his Porsche 911 Tur-burro."

HOMECOMINGS IN MONTREAL

It was always a good time when we traveled to Montreal to play the Expos. For me, it was like a homecoming, because so many people would make the short drive from Malone to watch our games.

I often left 50 or 60 tickets for everyone who made the 90-minute drive to Olympic Stadium. I remember my best friend, Mark, often making it out; my physics teacher; cross-country coach; some of the girls from school; and a lot of other friends who I hadn't seen in years came, too. It was pretty neat to see that I had an impact on so many people.

If I pitched well, everyone shared in the celebration after the game, buying me beers and congratulating me. And if I pitched poorly, I had dozens of people who could pick apart the game and tell me where I screwed up—whether I wanted them to or not. I didn't mind it, though. They were always great supporters, and it meant a lot to me that they wanted to be part of it.

I was proud that they were proud of me, and I was proud that I played a small part in putting Malone on the map.

KUNG FU FIGHTING

One of the biggest fights I was ever part of was against the New York Mets in 1986.

In the bottom of the ninth, Eric Davis stole third, and when he jumped up to his feet, he glanced Mets third baseman Ray Knight with an elbow. Knight responded with a right cross, and all hell broke loose.

Unfortunately for the Mets, they didn't know about our secret weapon: John Denny, who joined the club earlier that season.

Denny was one of the most aggressive guys I ever met, and he had a legendary temper. He brought over a martial-arts workout regimen that he and Steve Carlton used to use in Philadelphia, and he got Joe Price, Bill Gullickson, and me using it. We all felt like tough guys after a few weeks with the workout.

Well, the benches emptied, and it was just a big pile of players going at it. Kevin Mitchell, who was with the Mets at the time, was really going after guys, so Mario Soto went for his legs and I went high. We finally wrestled him to the ground, and then Denny released a barrage of shots to his stomach. Denny could seriously throw some punches, and he just let loose on Mitchell's gut. They said the poor guy was spitting up blood afterward.

Gary Carter then made the mistake of trying to corral Denny, who responded with something we called "The Claw." He'd grab your collarbone with one hand, and then he'd squeeze it until any movement you made caused paralyzing pain. It was a nasty, nasty clinch.

"Oh God!" screamed Mets coach Bill Robinson, seeing Denny with the grip. "No, John, no! No, no, no!"

Gary was completely frozen in his tracks. He couldn't move because of the lock John had on him. But after hearing the coach plead, John finally let go.

The brawl lasted for about 15 minutes, and I think everyone was involved in it at some point.

Everyone in the league hated the Mets that year because they were so good. But they knew it, and they were cocky about it. I think John Denny did that afternoon what the whole league had wanted to do all year.

RUBBER ARM

One of the few measuring sticks I used for my success was the number of starts I made and the number of innings I pitched each year.

I didn't have the "stuff" to register big strikeout totals, so I prided myself on my durability. In 1986 I started a league-high 39 games, and I led the league for the next three seasons after that. I also finished among the league leaders in innings pitched each of those seasons.

Eating innings was a matter of pride for me. In spring training, I always wanted to be the first guy to go five innings. And I always wanted to be the first guy to throw a complete game once the season started.

I knew I would never strike out batters at the rate someone like Mario Soto could, but it felt good knowing I could lead the league in something—other than the number of home runs allowed, of course.

OPENING DAY JITTERS

My first Opening Day start came in 1987. Pete told me in spring training that I was getting the honor. And trust me, it was a real honor. As a lifelong Reds fan and a major league pitcher, I couldn't imagine a better opportunity.

Cincinnati celebrates its openers like no other major league team. The city pretty much shuts down and focuses all of its attention on the Reds. For the players, it feels a lot like Christmas—it's hard to sleep, and you just can't wait until morning.

I watched the opener from the bench the year before when Mario Soto got the start. I knew it was a big deal for him. I knew he had to have been nervous, although he calmed down and pitched just fine.

But when I took the mound, the jitters never went away. I was really overwhelmed. It's one of the few times that the pressure and magnitude of a game really got to me.

We were playing Montreal in front of a sold-out crowd. Back then, Cincinnati always played the first game of the season, and we got a lot of national attention. Plus, it was my first opener as a starter, so the spotlight seemed 10 times brighter.

I struck out the first batter, Alonzo Powell, and the place went nuts. But I started getting tingly feelings in my legs, and everything soon felt like it was moving at twice the speed. I just could never catch up and collect myself, and the Expos ended up pounding me pretty good.

I was yanked after three innings. I was obviously disappointed, but I learned a lot that day about what it takes to control your emotions in a big game.

The day wasn't a complete wash, though. We came back for nine runs in the bottom of the fourth and ended up winning after Barry Larkin, Eric Davis, and Terry Francona all hit home runs.

In the years after that start, I pitched in a World Series and tossed a perfect game, but it took that horrible start on Opening Day to really prepare me for the pressure I would face in big games.

But that's Cincinnati for you. Only in the Queen City can you feel a true playoff atmosphere on the first day of the season.

E-MAN BOOGIE

I came up through the Reds farm system with Eric Davis. But in the minors, we called him "E-Man Boogie," or "Boogie" for short. I'm not sure exactly where the nickname came from, but even today, I have his phone number stored in my BlackBerry as "Boogie."

In 1987 he established himself as the next big thing in baseball. You often hear of guys being compared to history's greats, but when they said Boogie was the next Willie Mays, I just couldn't find a reason to disagree.

He won the NL Player of the Month award in both April and May, and put together some of the most remarkable streaks I'd ever seen. During a game in Philadelphia, he hit three home runs—one to left field, one to center, and one to right. He also leaped over the center field wall to rob Jack Clark of home runs in back-to-back games. And if it weren't for a late-season injury that year, he would have become baseball's first 40/40 guy.

It was just amazing to watch Boogie play. As a pitcher, there was no one I'd rather have playing center field.

It's a shame he had to fight through so many injuries. Some of it may have been because he didn't have an ounce of fat on his body, so he had no real cushioning to protect him. And some of it was probably because he just didn't know how to play any other way than all out.

Because of those injuries, Boogie never became the next Mays, Clemente, or Aaron like a lot of people predicted. His fortitude, though, was unquestionable. He overcame everything from a lacerated kidney to colon cancer to return to the starting lineup.

As far as I'm concerned, there was no more inspiring player than Boogie.

PETE'S WRATH

In mid-April 1987 I started feeling some tightness in my left forearm, right below the elbow. I had injured it during one of those martial-arts workouts with John Denny, but I was a rock-head and decided I could pitch through it. I just quit doing the workouts and assumed the pain would go away.

It was a bad decision.

I got my brains beat in for the next month. I really struggled and couldn't get any extension with my arm. But I refused to take an anti-inflammatory because, well, like I said, I'm a rock-head. When you're pitching on one-year contracts, you don't want to do anything to make the club question your health.

But it all came to a head on May 13. My ERA was huge, and I was rarely lasting more than five innings. We were playing in Montreal, and Mitch Webster hit a second-inning grand slam that gave the Expos a 6-0 lead.

That's when Pete yelled at me.

That wasn't really new. Pete would often raise his voice to get your attention, but then he'd talk to you to help you figure out what was going wrong. That day, though, Pete just yelled. He thought I was loafing it. He didn't think I was battling like I used to. He just seemed disgusted with me.

I was so frustrated, not just because I was hurting and struggling, but also because I felt like I let down my manager.

While doing some research for this book, I came across something interesting. The day of Pete's outburst was, according to the infamous Dowd Report, the exact day Pete's bookie refused to take any more of his bets.

I doubt his frustration with me resulted solely from his problems off the field, but it probably played a part in it. Pete was always a battler, and his intensity could often overcome any physical shortcomings. I think he saw a lot of himself in me, so he just wanted me to do the same. He was desperate to see me get back on track, but I never did.

I got pounded in my in my next four starts, and then they moved me to the bullpen, the one place I always dreaded. I made one relief appearance. I'm not sure if it was my ineffectiveness or the umpire's apparent refusal to call strikes, but Bo Diaz quit flashing me signs. He just told me to throw the ball and hope for the best.

Somehow, I pitched two scoreless innings, but management had already made up its mind: I was going back to the minors.

JUICED BALLS

Being sent to the minors was the low point of my career.

Pete called me into his office and said I was being sent to Class AAA Nashville. He told me not to read too much into it. He said he just wanted me to get myself straightened out, build up some confidence, and then come back to Cincinnati like my old self. I think it hurt him more than it did me, but I didn't really give him much of a choice.

"Just get yourself right, Puggy," he told me.

At that point, though, I really started second-guessing myself and questioned my ability to strike out major league hitters.

Plus, 1987 was the year of the juiced ball. Home run totals had never been so high. I remember pitching against the Phillies in May and little Luis Aguayo, a guy who had never hit more than a few home runs in a season, broke his bat, but still got a home run out of it. I also remember watching a highlight of Jack Howell or one of his teammates hitting a check-swing home run that year. It just seemed unbelievable to me. It felt like everyone was blasting away.

'Crack Of The Bat'
(THE NASHVILLE SOUND)

AAA STUDIOS

◄ AUDITIONS

GOSH, WHICH HIT SHALL I PLAY?
AFTER ALL, I'VE HAD SEVERAL!

BEST OF BROWNING 20-9 1985

TOO MANY HITS, TOM!

Two years after winning 20 games as a rookie, I was demoted to the minors. *The Cincinnati Enquirer* captured my mood pretty well. *Illustration courtesy Jerry Dowling*

As a pitcher, you hate seeing stuff like that. It makes you question the integrity of the game, and it affects your confidence. You second-guess everything.

So once I received word of my demotion, I concentrated on the one positive I could find in the whole mess. "At least I'll get away from that damn juiced ball," I told myself.

That optimism didn't last even one batter. The first batter I faced at Class AAA tagged me for a home run—the opposite-field variety, of course.

GETTING RIGHT

To be honest, I didn't realize that my demotion was the result of a physical problem. I assumed it was all psychological—a neck-up issue. I didn't realize how little extension I was actually getting with my arm.

Larry Doughty, the Reds' director of scouting, came down to Nashville to watch me toss in the bullpen. He said that mechanically I looked perfect, but that I usually had a little bit of a hitch in my delivery and that it was missing.

I got battered for another three starts before I finally agreed to take an anti-inflammatory. It helped almost immediately. I had a little more life on my fastball, and I felt like I was getting more extension.

And I felt ridiculous for not realizing it was a physical problem all along. Pride and stubbornness can be a bad mix.

I pitched well in my next start, and then I threw a complete-game shutout in the game that followed. I felt like I was back to my old self. I felt better physically, and my confidence was back.

Scotty Breeden, Cincinnati's pitching coach, made the trip to watch me pitch that last start. The Reds had an off-day, and he wanted to check on my progress. He walked into the trainer's room after the game with a smile on his face.

"How's it going, Tom?" he asked.

"Great, Scotty," I said. "I'm just ready to come home."

He just nodded his head in agreement.

"We're ready to have you."

They could have left me down there three more days, and I wouldn't have qualified for arbitration at the end of the year. I'm sure they realized it, but they called me up anyway. It cost them some money, but I wasn't stupid enough to question the timing.

I just wanted to go home.

STARVING FOR A CHANCE

My 1987 demotion ended up being one of the best things to ever happen to my career.

They say that getting to the majors is the easy part, but staying there is what's difficult. If you don't believe it, check out some Class AAA clubhouses. It's there that you'll find some of the hungriest ballplayers.

Once you get to the majors, you can really embrace the team concept. Everyone's working toward a single goal. In the minors, though, it's an environment in which you're forced to look out for yourself. You have to be selfish, hoping to steal someone's job as soon as they fail.

When I got to Nashville, I saw a locker room full of guys who would do anything to get a taste of the bigs. It was a wake-up call. If I didn't get myself headed in the right direction, I knew there were plenty of guys waiting to take my place.

DOCTOR'S APPOINTMENT

As humbled as I was during my demotion, I was twice as jubilant to be back in Cincinnati.

Pete didn't wait long to tell me I had an appointment with "the Doc"—the Mets' Dwight Gooden. I don't think they could have found a tougher opponent for me to face in my return. Gooden was perhaps the greatest pitcher in baseball at that time. Two years prior, he won the Cy Young Award after achieving the "pitcher's Triple Crown" by leading the league in wins, ERA, and strikeouts. The guy had the most amazing curveball you have ever seen. Ballplayers called a curveball "Uncle Charley" back then, but Gooden's was so good it was called "Lord Charles."

At the time, I was good friends with Ronnie Oester and his wife, Jackie. They were both happy to see me get back to Cincinnati, and as I would learn a few weeks later, Jackie actually went to church the morning of that game to say a prayer for me.

Her prayers—and mine—were answered. I felt completely healthy, I gave up just two runs in seven innings, and I left the game with a 7-2 lead.

It started to feel like a perfect ending to an otherwise terrible month, but fate sometimes had a weird way of working. In the top of the ninth inning, Mookie Wilson collided with Ronnie at second base. Ronnie's cleats got caught in the turf, and his leg buckled and broke. I always stuck around in the dugout after I left a game, so I got a front-row seat for the collision. It was one of the most horrific things I have seen. Ronnie was in tremendous pain, and you hate to see a teammate, especially such a good friend, have to experience something like that.

We ended up beating the Mets, and I got the win. But no one was celebrating afterward. It was just a bittersweet day, because I felt so guilty. I felt like I had stolen Ronnie's prayer.

BASEBALL STITCHES

In September that season, we headed to Candlestick Park to play the Giants, and I got the start in the first game of the series. The season was winding down, and I needed some quality outings. I still felt like I had something to prove since the demotion. It was a feeling that followed me throughout that year.

I went to bat in the second inning and drove a shot toward the foul line in left field. Joel Youngblood dove for the ball, but hit the wall and ended up breaking his wrist. But it wasn't the only injury in that at-bat.

On the very next pitch, Mike LaCoss threw a forkball that I swung at. I fouled it off the plate, and it shot up and hit me right in the nose.

I was dazed, and I tried to make it to our dugout, but I could see squirts of blood shooting out of the gash. They were little squirts timed perfectly with my heartbeat. I knew it wasn't good.

I threw off my helmet and crumbled to the ground. Doug Harvey, the home-plate umpire, came over to look at me. Only one thing entered my mind.

"Doug, there's no way I'm coming out of this game," I said. "No freakin' way. I've had a crappy year, and I've got a chance to win one. The season's almost over, and I'm running out of chances. I'm not leaving."

He must have thought I was knocked silly after hearing my tirade, but Doug was a world-class ump, and thankfully, he told me to take all of the time I needed.

Amazingly, a plastic surgeon just happened to be sitting next to our dugout. Security helped him over the fence, and right there on the field, he sewed me up with three stitches.

I stayed in the game, despite the broken nose, and the San Francisco fans gave me a nice round of applause. I thought I was Superman back then, but really, the pain wasn't all that bad.

I pitched another five innings, but I gave up some runs, and we lost. Bob Brenly was playing for the Giants that year, and he still tells me it's one of the toughest things he's seen from a ballplayer. I've seen guys play through a lot worse, but it's still a nice ego stroke.

TOILET HUMOR

I always appreciated and understood the role of veterans on a ball club, but that didn't keep me from screwing with the older guys from time to time. Of course, it usually came at the encouragement of my teammates.

During one of our trips to Chicago, our plane landed and we hopped on a bus to take us to the team hotel.

Dave Parker went into the restroom, and that's when Terry Francona thought it would be a good idea to lock him in there. Terry, of course, wouldn't do it himself, so he egged me on until I finally agreed to do it.

I took off my belt and wrapped it around a latch on the restroom door. I held onto the belt, pressed my back against a wall, and positioned my feet against the door to form an impenetrable brace.

Park pushed on the door, and it wouldn't budge.

"Let me out, you idiots," he said.

We hushed everyone so no one would laugh.

"Uh, I think the door's locked," I said. "Just make sure it's unlocked."

You could hear him jiggle it back and forth, and then he gave the door another push. It obviously didn't budge.

"I'm not kidding. Open the door!" he barked.

By this time, everyone had their faces buried in their hands, and it took everything we had to keep from laughing.

"Seriously man, there's not even a lock out here," I said. "Just give it a push."

Park pushed it, all right. And then he pounded on it. And then he slammed into the door. He was a huge guy, so everyone heard what was going on. Soon, it felt like the whole bus was rocking back and forth while Park went berserk.

At the first chance I got, I quickly unwrapped the belt from the door, hid it, and then took a seat while trying to sit as still as possible.

Park gave the door another shove, and it flew open. He must have seen about 30 guys sitting like they were frozen with their faces bright red and tears running down their cheeks.

He walked pretty calmly to the front of the bus to find Pete.

"Hey, Blockhead, you tell those guys I don't play like that," he said.

Park never said another word about the whole thing, but I know he thought twice before he ever used the bus restroom again.

SPRINGING LEAKS

No one was immune from the pranks in the clubhouse, not even the sportswriters.

Joe Minster, a writer from the *Hamilton Journal* and later the *Cincinnati Post*, was a favorite target, largely because he wore these awful super-wide ties, which we used to occasionally slice in half with scissors.

One day, Joe was interviewing Dave Parker by his locker. Johnny Franco decided to have a little fun and swiped a plastic syringe from the trainer's room. He filled it with water and shot little streams clear across the clubhouse at Joe's head. After each squirt, Joe would look up to try to find the leak, which he, of course, never found.

It would take everything we had to keep from laughing out loud every time Johnny soaked him.

It must have been a good 15 minutes before Joe finally gave up on the interview to head for drier land.

RESPECT FOR THE BACKSTOPS

I always had a good rapport with my catchers. It was probably because I understood how grueling the job can be and tried to make it as easy as possible for them.

Plus, there were two other reasons they loved me. One, I threw a ton of fastballs, so they didn't have to chase after many pitches. And two, I just didn't throw very hard.

I changed speeds often, and I hit my marks. That was about it. Catchers loved it.

My own catching career lasted just one pitch.

As an eight-year-old, I was given a catcher's mitt by my stepfather because our team needed a backstop. He figured I was the man for the job, but I hated it. The first pitch I tried to catch was fouled off and hit me in the knee. I hit the ground in pain, wondering how anyone could want that job. I immediately removed the equipment and demanded my regular spot in center field.

Once I got to the majors, I remember seeing guys like Bo Diaz, Jeff Reed, and Joe Oliver after games in the clubhouse. They'd be covered from head to toe in baseball-sized bruises, but you'd never hear them complain about how grueling the job was. I found some comfort in knowing I made their jobs at least a little easier on them.

THOSE CRAZY COEDS

A few times a year, the Reds offer discounted ticket prices for local college students. Back in the 1980s, the students would pack the place, and they were a wild bunch of kids. I'm sure beer sales were brisk.

I remember Dave Parker playing right field during one of those nights. Out of nowhere, a big purple dildo came flying down from the stands. The thing must have been two-feet long. It hit with a thud right behind Park and finally rolled to a stop on the warning track.

Once Park realized what it was, he had to cover his face with his glove so people couldn't see how hard he was laughing. I've seen games stopped many times because of debris on the field—beach balls, beer cups, even people. But that was definitely a first.

Park signaled for a ball boy and tossed him the projectile to take off the field.

I'm not sure if the kid knew what it what or what he was doing, but he clinched the thing right in the middle of its, well, "girth" and started running off the field. The thing started bouncing up and down as he ran, and with every step, the crowd roared with laughter.

We were just happy the thing never hit Dave and inflicted any damage. Could you imagine trying to explain that injury to the trainer?

ARBITRATION FRUSTRATION

After the 1987 season, I was arbitration-eligible, but my agent and I couldn't reach an agreement with the Reds, so I had to go to Chicago for a hearing.

Nobody wants to go through the arbitration process, especially a guy like me coming off a crappy year.

Basically, arbitration works like this: You submit a salary you think is fair, then the team submits a figure it feels is fair, and then an arbitrator rules in favor of one of you. There's no middle ground. You each plead your case, and either you win or the team wins.

Basically, club officials explain why you're a stiff, and you explain why they're idiots. That's why it's in everyone's best interest to reach an agreement beforehand. Hard feelings are inevitable. But after 1987, we just couldn't reach an agreement, so Reds general manager Murray Cook put together his case.

We entered a Chicago boardroom, and I heard a number of reasons why I stunk and didn't deserve the money I was requesting. It was hard not to take it personally. This was the team that drafted me and gave me a shot in the majors, and now they were explaining how I didn't even stack up with an average pitcher. But then they started comparing me to Kirby Puckett and guys who didn't even pitch, which seemed like a stretch. I started to think I had a good shot of winning.

I guess I was fortunate that we actually did settle before they ruled in anyone's favor. After Danny Jackson won his case, they decided they didn't want a big discrepancy between our two salaries because we were considered similar pitchers. So they budged on what they were offering, and my agent and I accepted.

I just wish we could have reached an agreement before we ever had a hearing. It's hard to hold back your anger when your team is trying to bury you. You want to yell out and defend yourself, but you really can't. But that's the way it works.

Today, I have a list of two things that I think any player needs for an arbitration hearing: thick skin and a short memory.

PESSIMISTIC ABOUT PARK

Prior to the 1988 season, our outfield was stocked with promising outfielders, including Eric Davis, Paul O'Neill, Kal Daniels, and Tracy Jones.

I don't think the front office saw a lot of room for an aging guy like Dave Parker, so he was shipped to Oakland. Cincinnati got Jose Rijo, a younger pitcher with a lot of promise, and Tim Birtsas, who was demoted to the minors the previous season and was kind of an unknown.

We all hated to see Park go. He had four amazing seasons with the Reds, and he provided a great presence in the clubhouse. He was a big reason the team turned around things in the mid-1980s.

I remember talking to one of my teammates about the trade and trying to look at the bright side.

"At least it looks like we're getting some good arms in return," I said.

But he didn't seem to share my optimism.

"Yeah, it's just too bad they're both on Rijo."

GEEK CHIC

When Buddy Bell got hurt during spring training in 1988, Chris Sabo unexpectedly left camp with the starting job at third.

I'm not sure which planet beamed "Sabes" down to Earth, but I'm glad they did. The guy was a little eccentric, but he was one heck of an aggressive competitor. And he wouldn't back down from anyone.

We went into Houston early in the year, and we were facing Nolan Ryan, one of baseball's last great intimidators and a hell of a fastball pitcher. Not that it mattered to Sabo.

He went to bat and struck out on three consecutive curveballs.

Once he got back to the dugout, he started yelling toward the mound. "Fastball, my ass! Why don't you challenge someone?"

Here I am thinking he's poking a bear, just asking to get plunked. But the next time Sabo went to bat, he got just what he asked for: Ryan struck him out on three straight fastballs.

He just walked casually to the dugout and announced, "Now, that's what I call a fastball!"

I just started laughing. The guy was in a world all his own.

Sabes, though, ended up having a fine season, winning National League Rookie of the Year honors. He reminded me a lot of Pete, but with more speed.

Sabes also had a cult-like following in Cincinnati that year. I must have seen thousands of Reds fans with Sabo-esque crew cuts and sports goggles at Riverfront Stadium that year.

ROSE VERSUS PALLONE

Our rivalry with the Mets came to a head again in April 1988. This time, I got ejected, and Pete earned a legendary suspension.

We were in the seventh inning and the Mets were up 4-2. Tim Teufel was due up, but he wasn't even in the batter's box when home-plate umpire Eric Gregg called a balk on me. I was incensed, and so was Pete. Technically, you can't even call a balk unless a batter is in the box, but we argued to no avail.

Afterward, Pete came out to the mound to talk to me.

"Look, Teufel hits you like he owns you anyway," he suggested. "Just go ahead and drill him if you want."

Pete read my mind. I could never seem to get Teufel out. I figured he was going to get to first base anyway, so I hit Teufel with the next pitch and at least kept him from him hitting a double. That got the Mets dugout riled up, and I was tossed from the game immediately.

I watched the rest of it from the clubhouse on television. The Reds came back to score some runs, and with the score tied 5-5 in the top of the ninth, Dave Pallone hesitated to call a Mets runner safe at first, which allowed the go-ahead run to score from second. Pallone had a history of controversial calls and ejections with Pete and Davey Concepcion, so the argument got really heated.

Pete ended up shoving Pallone with his elbow, but according to Pete, it was only after Pallone scratched him near his eye while they were both yelling and wagging their fingers at each other.

A lot of people questioned whether Pallone really caught Pete with his finger. But after he got tossed and came into the clubhouse, which is where I was after my ejection, I saw Pete, and he had a visible cut by his eye. To see Pete react like that, I knew he had to have been provoked.

After the incident, Pete got hosed by Bart Giamatti, the National League president. He suspended Pete for 30 days and fined him $10,000. It was the most severe punishment for anything a manager had ever done on the field, and I knew it was far too harsh.

I think the thing that made Pete most upset wasn't losing or the personal grudge he had toward Pallone. That day, Pete just felt like his guys didn't get a fair shake. He didn't think New York beat us legitimately, and as manager of the club, he felt like he had to do something to stand up for us. It's a shame he had to pay such a steep price for it.

AMAZING GRACE AND DANNY

I had one of my best seasons in 1988, even though I didn't get my first win until May 10. After the slow start, though, I went 18-5 with a 3.41 ERA. But I was only the second-best pitcher on the team that year.

Danny Jackson, who came over from Kansas City, had an absolutely astounding season. He threw a hard, heavy sinker and broke more bats that year than any pitcher I had ever seen. He went 23-8 and finished second in voting for the NL Cy Young Award to Orel Hershiser, who closed out the season with an unbelievable 59 straight scoreless innings.

During that season, you may have seen Danny and I flash each other three fingers from time to time. After getting out of a jam or getting a big win, we'd hold up our hands with three fingers pointing upward.

The tradition originated while we were on the road in Philadelphia and I was watching a movie on HBO called *Amazing Grace and Chuck*. Two of the main characters would flash each other the sign, which was supposed to symbolize their unity or something like that. Danny just happened to be watching the movie at the same time I was, and we talked about it in the clubhouse later that day. So we adopted the sign as kind of joke, but it stuck. We used it throughout the season, and it came to really symbolize our season together.

Fourteen years after that season, the Reds had closing ceremonies for Cinergy Field, which was going to be imploded later that year to make room for Great American Ball Park.

A lot of former players who called the stadium home got invited to the festivities, including Danny and me. When we got announced to the crowd, each guy would shake hands with the others who were standing on the foul line. Instead of shaking hands, though, Danny and I of course opted for our three-finger salute.

CY CONCEPCION

Every pitcher thinks he can play in the field, and every position player thinks he can pitch. That's just the way it is.

Against the Dodgers one time in 1988, Davey Concepcion finally got his chance.

We were getting pounded and had gone through a ton of pitchers, so Pete let Davey take the mound for the last inning and a third. He gave up a couple hits but no runs, and he even struck out a guy.

After the game, Davey was strutting around the clubhouse like he was Cy Young. Never mind the fact that we had just gotten beat by like 10 runs. But when a position player finally gets a chance like that, you just have to let them bask in the glory.

I didn't have the heart to tell Davey that he didn't throw hard enough to break a pane of glass. Besides, he threw one of the better "gravity balls" I had ever seen.

RIVERFRONT ALL-STARS

Riverfront Stadium played host to the All-Star Game in 1988. And as far as I was concerned, if I wasn't going to be in the game, I at least wanted to go and watch it.

The Reds arranged for my wife and me to get a couple of seats in right field. We settled in to watch Barry Larkin, Danny Jackson, and Chris Sabo, the Reds' All-Star representatives that year. Being their teammate, I was definitely proud to see the guys get the recognition they deserved.

Sabo was just a rookie that year, but he already had a huge following in Cincinnati, and he was quickly becoming the darling of the national media. There was just something naturally likeable about the guy.

Like Pete, he just didn't look like a ballplayer, so I think fans loved to root for him. He was kind of the underdog of the team. No one expected him to make the club out of camp, and at 26 years old, he just wasn't your typical rookie.

In the seventh inning, they sent Sabo into the game to pinch run. The place started getting louder, and when he took off to steal second, 55,000 people jumped to their feet. Sabes was called safe, and the place celebrated like the Reds had just won the World Series.

I had pitched in front of a huge Opening Day crowd the year before, and I knew the only place that was probably louder than the pitcher's mound that day was second base. I'm sure it was probably a pretty amazing experience for Sabo. The guy went from being a nobody in spring training to an All-Star hero in just four months.

TOUGH LOAF

If there's one thing Pete didn't tolerate, it was his players loafing it.

We were playing the Padres at home toward the end of the 1988 season. They had tagged me for a couple of runs, and I made the mistake of trying to feel sorry for myself.

I went to bat in the third inning, and I hit a rocket to third base, but Chris Brown dove to knock it down. I hit it hard, but I knew I was beat, so my sprint to first turned into a jog once I was about 10 feet from the bag.

Brown, though, had trouble getting the ball out of his glove. I didn't know it, because I never looked back over there. I was getting closer and closer to first, and the ball still wasn't there. Finally, right before I got to the bag, Carmelo Martinez caught, and I was out by a hair.

Once I got to the dugout, Pete chewed me out.

"You never stop running! Never!" he yelled. "You cost us an out!"

Tony and Davey chewed me out, too. And rightfully so. I deserved it. I had been in the majors long enough to know better than to let up like that, and it was a veteran's job to remind me when I screwed up.

And I never loafed like that again.

ART OF BEAN BALLS

A lot of people don't understand the concept of bean balls, not even players.

I intentionally hit very few people in my career, but if I did, I usually had a good reason. But you just don't start plunking everyone you have a problem with or don't like.

I remember Darryl Strawberry bragging before a game one time that I didn't have the "guts" to hit him. This was during our bitter rivalry with the Mets, so there was a lot of trash talking going on at the time.

We ended up winning the game 3-1, and he was right, I didn't hit him. But it wasn't because I didn't have the guts. It just didn't make any sense at the time. I'm not going to risk blowing a lead just to settle some petty score.

Winning always took precedence over getting even.

RUNNING FOR MY LIFE

I always loved running.

I also had this theory that it flushed out the bad blood around my shoulder and elbow and circulated fresh blood into those areas. And just as importantly, it really gave me some time to work out my problems mentally to clear my mind after a bad game.

I have no doubt that it's one of the best things a pitcher can do between starts, and I'm surprised more guys don't do it today.

In most cities, I had routes I ran in the neighborhoods around the ballparks or near the hotels where we stayed. Running along Lake Michigan in Chicago and through the streets of San Francisco, Philadelphia, and San Diego provided some amazing scenery.

In Cincinnati, I had a nice half-hour course from Pete Rose Way into Newport and Covington and back into Riverfront.

One of the few bad experiences I ever had while running was in Atlanta near Fulton County Stadium. The neighborhood looked safe enough, but I was probably no more than a couple blocks into my run when I came upon the most god-awful barking I had ever heard. It was getting closer and closer to me. I turned around and saw a big pit bull tearing after me.

I was scared to death. This thing looked like he wanted to chew a chunk out of me. He chased me for blocks, and it took everything I had to stay ahead of him. Every time I thought about letting up, I'd turn around and see him getting closer and closer. After what felt like an hour, though, he finally tired out and turned around for home. But it was the last time I ever ran outside the stadium in Atlanta.

CAPTAIN UNDERPANTS

We used to call Rob Murphy "Captain Yum Yum" back in the 1980s.

The pitchers used to throw the team parties at the end of the year, and one time Murph went all out. He got a black mask and cape, and he came out wearing nothing else but black skivvies. That's when someone came up with the nickname.

Soon after, Murph always wore black underwear when he pitched. He was really superstitious, and he thought they brought him good luck.

You could always count on him for comic relief like that.

Well, you could count on him for pitching relief, too.

The guys in the bullpen used to keep a little list they checked off every time one of them was called to warm up. One year Murph had well over 120 ticks next to his name, which meant they considered using him three out of four games that year. It's just a staggering number to consider.

It wasn't uncommon for Murph to end up appearing in more than half the games we played in a season. He was the main setup guy for John Franco, but he never got the praise he deserved for his durability.

7

PERFECT PONDERINGS

A PERFECT MINDSET

I often get asked about my perfect game, and at one point on September 16, 1988, I started thinking it could become a reality.

People probably think I'm just being modest when I say that pitchers really don't think about that type of stuff. But really, we don't.

If you worry about pitching a no-hitter or perfect game every time you take the mound, you're going to be disappointed 99.999 percent of the time. So you just concentrate on getting hitters out and giving your team a chance to win.

That's not to say that kind of stuff didn't used to enter my mind. Back during my rookie season, I was pitching against the Cardinals and took a no-hitter into the fifth or sixth inning, but Cesar Cedeño led off the inning with a double. He was thrown out trying to stretch it into a triple, so I was at third base backing up Buddy Bell.

As I walked back to the mound, I looked over at Buddy and told him my no-hitter was gone.

"Quit worrying about that crap," he said. "Just worry about pitching. We all still have a ballgame to win."

He made me realize how selfish I sounded. I had eight other guys on the field trying to win a ballgame, and I was moping about my own bad luck.

I took Buddy's advice to heart, and after that, I just really tried not to think about no-hitters and perfect games. I just concentrated on winning games.

ALMOST ROBBY

Four months before my perfect game, it was a different Reds pitcher who nearly made history.

Ron Robinson was just one strike away from his own perfect game when Montreal pinch hitter Wallace Johnson, a guy who had just a few at-bats all season, connected for a single on 2-2 pitch with two outs in the bottom of the ninth.

Robby couldn't have possibly gotten any closer to a perfect game. He was just one strike away.

I felt terrible for him.

It's hard to say anything to a guy after something like that. There are no words that could possibly make things better. Instead, you just get the hell out of the guy's way.

What made the performance so much more remarkable was the pain he was pitching with. Robby had arm troubles all year. His elbow was in such bad shape that he would have to squat down to pick up the ball from the mound. He just couldn't straighten out his arm to reach down and pick it up.

I don't know how he was able to pitch like that. Guts and guile and whatever else he could muster, I suppose. But he had simply wonderful stuff that night, and I was really hoping he'd pull it out.

Even when I was just one strike away from my own perfect game, I'm sure Robby's game was still fresh in everyone's minds.

LOOKING FOR REDEMPTION

The night of my perfect game was actually a rematch of sorts. Five days prior, I was facing Tim Belcher and the Dodgers at their place.

With the game scoreless in the third inning, Belcher came to the plate. Like most pitchers, he wasn't much of a hitter.

I quickly got ahead and worked the count to 0-2.

I then threw a ball under his shins and about six inches inside. It was a perfect 0-2 pitch. It was un-hittable as far as I was concerned. If he was dumb enough to swing at it, there's no way he was going to get wood on it.

That's what I thought anyway.

Instead, Belcher golfed a shot to left field for a home run.

After the inning, Pete asked me how in the hell I served up a home run—to a pitcher—on an 0-2 count. To this day, I still say it was a good pitch.

"Pete, the pitch was on the ground," I pleaded. "There's no way he should have hit it. It wasn't a bad pitch. He got lucky."

I ended up leaving the game with a lead, but we lost in the bottom of the ninth.

So when the Dodgers and Belcher came to Cincinnati and I got my rematch, I, of course, felt like I had something to prove, and I had redemption on my mind. I wanted to put my previous loss behind me, and there was no better way to do that than shutting down the Dodgers the second time around.

I wasn't thinking about a perfect game. I was just thinking about revenge. And besides, it was the Dodgers. And I hated the Dodgers.

CRUMMY CONDITIONS

I didn't think we were going to play at all the night of the perfect game.

It was a horrible day. It rained all afternoon and evening, and it didn't look like it was going to stop.

At 7:35 p.m., the game was officially delayed. I just hung out in the dugout and tried to keep myself loose. I didn't really talk to anyone on the days I pitched, so everyone just pretty much left me alone so I could concentrate.

At one point, I walked up to the dugout to take a look at the field. Through the downpour, I saw Tim Belcher in the Dodgers dugout. He must have been checking out the conditions, too.

I gave him a tip of the cap, and he did the same to me. It was just kind of a silent acknowledgment of each other. We both stood there and watched it rain for a little while before heading back to the clubhouse.

By 9:30 p.m., I figured the game was a wash, and I began to undress and put my street clothes back on. But one of the guys from the grounds crew came in and said that the weather forecast was showing a small window at 10 p.m. and that we could probably squeeze the game in. It was late in the season, and we weren't sure there would be an opportunity for a makeup game, so the umpires decided we'd play.

I still wonder how close they came to postponing the game. If it was earlier in the season and we had a chance to make it up sometime later, the game probably would have been called.

And I probably wouldn't be writing this chapter.

RIVER PEOPLE

Once I heard that the game would start at 10 p.m., I fell into my normal pregame routine. At 9:40 p.m., I began my walk to the bullpen. I finished stretching by 9:43 p.m., and I threw my first warmup pitch at 9:44 p.m.

It was the same routine I had been using for as long as I can remember.

The only difference was the stadium. As I walked onto the field, I took a look around the place. It was really quiet and kind of dark that night.

The thing that really caught my attention was the crowd—or actually, the complete lack of one. By the time I got to the field, there were only a few thousand fans left. Although the official paid attendance that night was 16,000 or so, the actual attendance was much lower.

It was September, and we were pretty much out of the playoff race. And then there was the two-and-a-half-hour rain delay. We figured they had to drag people out of the Ohio River and out from under the bridges to get them to come into the stadium on a night like that. That's why we called them "river people."

In the years since that game, I've been amazed by the number of people who have introduced themselves and said they were there that night. By my count, I've met every river person—at least three or four times.

A PERFECT OPPONENT

It took us maybe 40 minutes to get through the first five innings of the game that night. But that wasn't all that unusual. After all, I always worked quickly.

But as solid as I was that night, Tim Belcher was equally impressive for the Dodgers. As we entered the sixth inning, Belcher had a no-hitter of his own. He was matching me out for out, and he looked just as sharp as I did.

One of the biggest reasons a perfect game never really entered my mind until very late in the night was because of Belcher. It was impossible to think about a no-hitter or a perfect game if we couldn't score any runs. Retiring 27 straight wouldn't make a lick of difference if we didn't have at least one run on the board.

Looking back, I guess I can now understand the frustration that a guy like Harvey Haddix must have experienced. Back in the 1950s, he pitched nine perfect innings, but because the Pirates hadn't scored any runs for him, they had to go into extra innings. Haddix continued pitching, but ended up losing it in the 13th, and according to Major League Baseball, it doesn't qualify as a perfect game because he got the loss. Talk about tough luck.

I was only in the sixth inning, though, so I wasn't feeling that type of desperation quite yet. But with each out I recorded, I knew the need for a run was getting greater. Not for the perfect game, but just to get the win.

ALL BY MYSELF

Pitching a perfect game can be a pretty lonely experience.

Once the guys in the dugout realize you're getting close, you can't pay a guy to talk to you. No one wants to be the one to break your concentration or jinx you, so you're left there all by yourself. No pats on the back. No words of encouragement. Nothing.

I was never really big into that type of superstition, but I knew better than to start talking to anyone in the dugout. I would have felt horrible if we blew the perfect game or no-hitter and one of my teammates thought it was his fault.

Still, though, I always laugh when I think about Don Larsen's perfect game in the 1956 World Series. I've read stories about him walking up and down the bench that day asking each of his teammates, "Can you believe it? Can you believe I've got a perfect game going?"

Apparently, he wasn't the superstitious type either.

For me, it probably started in the sixth inning. I was sitting at the end of the bench in my usual spot. I remember looking down at the other side of dugout, and no one would even make eye contact with me.

It got worse as we got later in the game. I would look down the bench and stare at guys for a few minutes. I knew they could see me out of the corner of their eyes, but they wouldn't look. Guys like Paul O'Neill and Nick Esasky were just squirming in their seats while I stared at them. I knew it was making them uncomfortable, so it was actually pretty funny.

I could understand it, though. Being part of a no-hitter or a perfect game isn't just about the pitcher. Everyone wants to be part of one. Everyone wants to be able to say they were there and had a hand in it, whether it was recording outs or scoring a run.

I don't think anyone believes they can really jinx something like that. But with the stakes so high, nobody's willing to take that chance.

LARK TO THE RESCUE

The game was nearly two-thirds complete, and we were still scoreless. Belcher and I hadn't allowed a single hit, and I was starting to feel the pressure.

Ronnie Oester grounded out to lead off the bottom of the sixth, and then I hit a grounder to the pitcher for the second out.

We were then at the top of the order, and Barry Larkin came to the plate with two outs. Barry had a great first half that year, but had started to slow down a bit in the second. He had scored and knocked in just a couple runs all month, but still, he was one of the best leadoff hitters in the game that year. Barry was just as likely to get on base as anyone in the league.

On cue, Barry laced a double down the right field line, and I thought we were in business. Belcher's no-hitter was gone, and we had a runner in scoring position. I think Belcher even got a nice round of applause for his efforts.

Chris Sabo then came to bat, and I was hoping for any type of base hit. I figured Barry had enough speed to score on just about anything hit to the outfield.

Instead, he grounded a shot to third base. The ball, though, took a weird bounce. I think it hit the area between the turf and the dirt, Jeff Hamilton, the third baseman, eventually corralled it, but threw low to first base. Mickey Hatcher tried to scoop the ball, but it popped up about 20 feet in the air. As he waited for it to come back down and play it off the hop, Larkin charged around third to try to score.

I figured it was going to be a close play at the plate, but the ball kicked dead left on Hatcher once it touched down. It must have had some weird spin on it. Hatcher had no shot at Larkin, who crossed home plate well ahead of the throw.

"Well, there's your lead," I said to myself.

It was an unearned run, but it was a run nonetheless. The crowd celebrated our slim lead, and I just concentrated on the nine remaining outs.

STOP SIGNS

When I entered the seventh inning, I was facing the top of Dodgers lineup for the third time. That's when it kind of hit me that I just needed to get everyone out one more time.

And that's when the excitement got to me. I just wanted to mow them down right away.

But Pete thought that's when I usually got in the most trouble. I always worked quickly, but if I worked too quickly, he thought that I had a tendency to throw it right over the plate.

Jeff Reed, my catcher that night, told me after the game that Pete was worried about it. Pete continually signaled to Jeff from the dugout, telling Jeff to slow me down. He'd try to buy some time between pitches, fiddling with the ball and standing up to stretch his legs before he'd throw it back to me. Occasionally, he'd just raise both his hands and signal for me to slow down.

That night, though, everything clicked. My command was awesome. I hit all my marks. The ball went exactly where I wanted it to go. If I did throw one down the middle, guys either fouled it off or didn't swing. Everything was going my way.

Only rarely do you feel that type of invincibility on the mound. And when it happens, you can't pitch quickly enough.

SEEING ISN'T BELIEVING

The last batter I faced in the top of the seventh inning was Kirk Gibson.

I had retired Alfredo Griffin and Mickey Hatcher, and by that time, the crowd was really into it. Most of the fans had settled into the blue seats between first and third base—and God bless them—they cheered with all their might and almost made it sound like a full house that night.

I worked the count to 2-2 on Gibson, and then I threw one on the outside corner. Home-plate umpire Jim Quirk signaled a called strike three, and that's when Gibson went nuts.

He threw the back of his wrist on his hip, just like Pete used to do when he didn't agree with a call. He pointed to the edge of the plate with his bat and started screaming and shaking his head at the umpire.

I began walking back to the dugout, so I didn't really pay much attention to what was going on. It was only after the crowd reacted that I realized Gibson has been ejected from the game.

In fairness to Gibson, I think the plate did widen a bit toward the end of the game. Maybe it was a generous called strike, but if it's a close pitch on a two-strike count (during a perfect game, nonetheless), you have to swing, as far as I'm concerned.

Kirk, obviously, didn't agree. He thought Quirk was a little too generous with the calls that night.

Even today when Kirk is asked about the perfect game, his response is usually the same.

"What do I think about the perfect game?" he'll say. "I wouldn't know. I've never seen one."

THREE TO GO

We breezed through the eighth inning fairly quietly, and after Belcher retired our guys, I took the mound for what I hoped would be the final three outs.

Inside, I was a wreck. I was as nervous as nervous could be. I was just trying to keep my composure. Not only because of the perfect game, but because we had a slim lead, it was the Dodgers, and I at least wanted the shutout.

Rick Dempsey led off the inning with a fly ball down the right field line. He gave it a ride, but Paul O'Neill tracked it down with little trouble.

Steve Sax then hit a first pitch up the middle that Barry Larkin easily got to. Two outs.

Tracy Woodson then pinch-hit for Belcher. A few months prior, Ron Robinson's near-perfect game was spoiled with one strike to go—by a pinch hitter. If it was a bad omen, I was too nervous to notice.

Woodson was now the only thing standing between me and a perfect game.

The crowd was on its feet. You would have thought 50,000 people were there.

I quickly fell behind 2-0. It was funny, though. Neither of those pitches was close to the strike zone, but the crowd booed as though Jim Quirk had committed some cardinal sin for calling them balls. You gotta love hometown crowds.

But I bounced back for a called strike. And then Woodson fouled one off.

The count was 2-2. One strike was all I needed.

I threw a pitch, and it was supposed to go high and inside. But it went really high. And for reasons I'll never understand, he felt obligated to swing.

Strike three.

Game over.

Perfect game.

SAW IT HERE FIRST

After that last out, that's when I let it all go. All of those emotions came pouring out.

I pumped my fist and then gave it "The Saw"—a quick arm action that looks like you're sawing through a log. Man, I loved that feeling.

But remember Kirk Gibson, the guy who was tossed from the game and says he has never seen a perfect game? What do you think he did a few weeks later when he hit that legendary Game 1 home run in the 1988 World Series? The one where he had to hobble around the bases because his knees were so bad? Yup, he too gave it "The Saw."

Remember, though: You saw it in Cincinnati first.

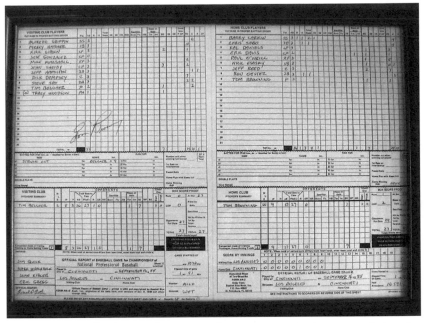

Ronald Roth, the official scorer during my perfect game, says that his scorecards from that night are some of his prized possessions. *Photo courtesy of Dann Stupp*

TIME TO CELEBRATE

Within seconds of that last out, everyone in a Reds uniform swarmed to the pitcher's mound for a ruckus like I'd never seen.

The infielders got to me first, and then Ronnie Oester and I fell to the ground while everyone else piled on.

Pinned between the turf and a couple thousand pounds of my teammates, I found myself lying on the ground face to face with Ronnie.

"Do you know what you just did!" he yelled. "Huh, do you? You just threw a f----- perfect game! A perfect game!"

I was nearly speechless—but not because I couldn't find the words to respond.

"Yeah, I know," I said, struggling to breathe. "But man, this pile is getting heavy!"

Soon, everyone peeled off, and I didn't look like a guy who pitched a perfect game. Instead, I looked like a guy who just went 12 rounds.

During the celebration, my lip was busted wide open, my whole body had been crushed, and I was covered in dirt and mud.

It didn't matter, though. I had enough adrenaline rushing through my body for 20 guys my size.

My teammates then hoisted me onto their shoulders. And although I was only five or six feet off the ground, it felt like 20. You talk about an out-of-body experience, well, that was one. It was like I was floating above the whole thing and looking down on it. Everything was so surreal.

As far as personal accomplishments go, it doesn't get much better than that. But to share it with a team and create that type of atmosphere for everyone to enjoy—well, that's what makes it so perfect.

STAR OF THE GAME

After the game, I did a bunch of interviews with the media guys down on the field. I don't even remember what they asked or what I said. I was still pretty much in a state of shock.

It went on for about a half hour before I thought I was all finished. I started to head back to the clubhouse, and that's when I saw Joe Nuxhall running after me with a microphone.

Back then, Joe did the "Star of the Game" segment after each game for the radio broadcast, and he wanted to do a quick interview with me before I left.

At Riverfront Stadium, the only way to get on the field back then was through a small door right behind home plate. It had a very low overhang, and you had to duck to keep from getting clocked in the head.

But Joe must have been swept up by the moment. He had a huge smile on his face when he saw me. He ran straight for the door, but never ducked. His head smacked the concrete block, and he was knocked right on his butt. One moment, the Ol' Left-hander was charging straight for me, and the next moment his legs were kicked up in the air and he was on his back.

I was afraid my perfect game had just killed a Cincinnati icon. But I ran over to find him lying on the ground, bright red and laughing hysterically.

Luckily, Nuxy wasn't hurt, just knocked a little silly.

```
                                                    ⌐TB
                                                     File

PROG-ID    WVQUMH       MAJOR LEAGUE BASEBALL           DATE  9/19/88
PAGE NO    2  USER-REDS     * MESSAGE LISTING *   MODE-*NEW TIME 15.44.26


   PERFECT GAME                                        FROM-KATY
           SENT- 9/19/88 15:22:29          RCVD- 9/19/88 15:44:27

   Tom Browning
   Cincinnati Reds
   100 Riverfront Stadium
   Cincinnati, OH 45202

   Dear Mr. Browning:

   Congratulations on your perfect game last Friday.  It was a tremendous
   feat, especially considering the long rain delay, and places you among
   elite company in baseball history. Best of luck the rest of the way.

   A. Bartlett Giamatti
   President, National League


   NOTE: Please deliver above message to Mr. Browning.  Thank you.
```

National League president Bart Giamatti used baseball's electronic messaging system to send his well wishes after my perfect game. *Photo courtesy of Tom Browning*

NO BO

Jeff Reed was my catcher the night of the perfect game, and he did a phenomenal job, especially considering what was at stake in the later innings.

But he wasn't my usual catcher that year.

If it weren't for his season-ending knee surgery in August, Bo Diaz probably would have been the guy catching that night.

It still pains me thinking about Bo after the game. He actually apologized to me for being hurt and not catching that night. I could see a real sense of remorse in his eyes, even though we both knew there was nothing he could do about his knee.

It was almost like Bo felt guilty for being hurt and not being there. We had forged a close relationship over the years, and honestly, he really deserved to be part of the perfect game because he was a big reason for my success back then.

I think Bo knew right away that he missed out on a historic moment. Only a few guys could say they ever caught a perfect game, and Bo missed his chance.

All things considered, though, I couldn't have asked for a better replacement in Jeff. But it's still a little tough when I look back at the pictures of the celebration after the final out. It just feels like something's missing because Bo wasn't there with me.

JAM JOB

One memento I kept from the perfect game was a ball from the seventh inning. It didn't have any real significance to the game, though. I just thought it was something cool that had happened.

I was facing Mickey Hatcher in the top of the seventh, and I threw a fastball in on his hands. It was a jam job from hell.

Hatcher, though, managed to nub a pop up to Nick Esasky at first. Once they tossed the ball around the infield and got it back to me, I took a look. Hatcher was using a black bat with a silver Louisville Slugger logo, and I jammed him so hard, the silver rubbed off to make a perfect reverse logo on the ball.

I wanted to show Pete how badly I got into Hatcher's kitchen, so I rolled the ball into the dugout for him. I didn't make a big deal about it. In fact, Pete and I were probably the only ones who even noticed. But I knew he'd find it funny. Pete studied the intricacies of the game more than I anyone I knew, so I knew he'd appreciate how good a pitch that was.

After the game, one of the ball boys came up to me and asked if I wanted any of the balls that were used that night. During the course of a game, a lot of balls are discarded if they become cut or scuffed. They usually throw them off the field, and we end up using them for batting practice. That night, though, I guess you could say all the discarded balls had some historical significance.

I ended up taking six or seven for friends and family, including the one I used to jam Hatcher. I gave the ball to my dad after the season, and I'm sure he still has it. He was a pitcher back in his playing days, so I knew he'd get a kick out of its significance.

DOMINATING STUFF

I never considered the possibility of pitching a perfect game, even after I took a few no-hitters late into games.

To pitch a perfect game, I assumed a pitcher would need a big fastball or a really dominating pitch. But I usually pitched hoping that the batter would make contact. I didn't strike out a lot of guys. I just tried to trick them and get them to swing at bad pitches.

But on the night of the perfect game, I have to admit that I was pretty dominant. Of my 102 pitches, 72 were thrown for strikes. I never went to three balls on a single batter. In fact, I think the longest at-bat came against Jeff Hamilton after he fouled off four or five pitches.

For the most part, they were all pretty easy, routine outs.

That night, I almost felt like a different pitcher. I just felt like I couldn't do anything wrong.

And I got a taste of what it's like to be one of those overpowering and dominating pitchers. And it felt good.

PERFECTLY QUIET

Back in 2002, *The Cincinnati Enquirer* listed its top 100 moments in Cinergy Field history. The stadium was scheduled for an implosion, so the whole city was feeling a bit nostalgic.

Of all the great moments to choose from—the Big Red Machine, Pete Rose, the 1990 World Series, and plenty more—the newspaper actually ranked the perfect game as the ninth greatest event in stadium history.

I've always found it ironic that the game has gotten so much attention over the years, especially when you consider how quietly it happened.

Because of the rain delay and late start, the Dodgers ended up canceling their television broadcast that night. The Reds didn't broadcast it on TV either. And thanks to the two-hour rain delay, I'm guessing a lot of the radio listeners ended up tuning out.

By the time the game was finished, it was after midnight, and most people were probably asleep. I doubt the majority of Reds fans even knew about it until the next day.

However, in the years since, it's earned more than its fair share of attention, including displays in the Reds Hall of Fame, a banner outside Great American Ball Park, and even a mayor-proclaimed "Tom Browning Day" every September 16 in the city of Cincinnati.

COOPERSTOWN COLLECTION

I knew pretty early in my career that I wasn't Cooperstown material. But I think probably every player has a secret desire to somehow become associated with the National Baseball Hall of Fame and Museum.

During events like Pete's record-breaking hit and Eric Davis's three grand slams in a month, representatives from Cooperstown came looking for items to add to their collection. It's a great service, really—preserving the history of the game and all.

After the perfect game, I finally got to experience it for myself. I was both thrilled and humbled to hand over a cap and game ball from the perfect game for Cooperstown to add to its collection.

Although I'm not a Hall of Famer, I can always say I found my way into Cooperstown.

DELAYED CELEBRATION

Bill Gullickson was one of my best friends in baseball, so it meant a lot that he called me soon after the perfect game.

In 1988, he was pitching for the Tokyo Giants, but he heard about the game clear overseas in Japan just a few hours after it happened.

It was 5 a.m. when he called. He was probably more excited than I was. He couldn't wait to talk about it. He wanted to know everything that happened that night.

```
    +
    IPM070H
    4-01777LS261  09/17/88
    ICS IPMMTZZ CSP
    ZCZC  2123717800 FRS TDMT NEW YORK NY 9 09-17 1241P EST
    PMS TOM BROWNING, DLR
    CARE JIM FERGUSON, DLR
    CINCINNATI REDS
    100 RIVERFRONT STADIUM
    CINCINNATI OH 45202

    BT

    CONGRATULATIONS ON YOUR HISTORY MAKING PERFORMANCE.

    BEST PERSONAL REGARDS,
       PETER V UEBERROTH

    NNNN
    1239 EST
    +
    IPM070H
```

In traditional baseball fashion, baseball commissioner Peter Ueberroth sent his congratulations, via Western Union, after my perfect game. *Photo courtesy of Tom Browning*

That was the first time I had ever talked with someone overseas. There's a small delay from the time you talk until the person on the other end actually hears you.

Gully and I were going back and forth, cutting each other off because of the delay.

"Can you believe it, can you—"

"What was it like? Can you believe—"

"Huh, go ahead. I was just saying—"

"Wait, what? Huh, no, go ahead—"

"The rain delay, man, I thought it was—"

"Sorry. Wait, what? You go ahead—"

We were just so excited. I doubt we had two consecutive sentences with no interruptions for the first half of the conversation. It took us a while before we both calmed down and had a normal conversation.

The call probably ended up taking three or four times longer because of those delays. But what did I care? I wasn't paying for the call.

A BETTER WOMAN

The day after the perfect game, Marge Schott called Debbie and said she wanted to see Debbie and the kids at the game.

Marge was always wonderful to the players' wives. She wanted them to feel appreciated and part of the team, and she was especially fond of Deb.

I met them all in Marge's office that afternoon, and I figured she had something really special planned. The sentimental Reds owner could never let a major accomplishment go unrewarded.

I'm not sure Marge even completely understood the significance or the rarity of something like a perfect game, but she obviously knew it was something worth making a fuss over.

She smiled and handed me, as she explained it, "a perfect rose for my perfect pitcher." The stemmed rose wasn't exactly a Corvette like Pete got when he broke Ty Cobb's record, but I didn't really expect something like that. Pete's record was 23 years in the making, and I just had a fluke two-hour game. But I was still a little confused by the whole thing.

Marge's biggest surprise, though, was yet to come.

She directed her attention to my wife and pulled out a big white box from behind her desk.

One of the "famous dates banners" outside Great American Ball Park pays tribute to September 16, 1988, the day of my perfect game. *Photo courtesy of Dann Stupp*

"Debbie, behind every great man, there's an even better woman," she said with smirk. "Go ahead and open it."

Debbie opened the box, and pulled out a beautiful full-length mink coat.

Debbie was ecstatic and thanked Marge. I think she even got a little teary-eyed. Marge just smiled and then looked over at me.

"Are you upset, honey?" she asked.

"Of course not," I said. "I'm just happy I don't have to buy her one."

TWO MINUTES OF FAME

A few days after the perfect game, I was asked to be on one of those national morning TV shows. I think it was *Good Morning America.*

Now, I've pitched in front of some pretty crowds, and I had even pitched in front of some national TV audiences. But I never really got nervous when it came to pitching. However, doing a sit-down interview with my big mug filling up the entire screen was more than a little nerve-racking. Pitching was easy. Sounding insightful and witty wasn't.

Deb and I made it to the Cincinnati affiliate station at about 6 a.m. so we could go on at 6:10 a.m. The butterflies were in my stomach, and soon the lights flickered on and I was being beamed all over the country.

I was asked a few cupcake questions, and I started to get into the interview. But less than two minutes later, it was over.

"That's it?" I thought.

By my calculations, I was still 13 minutes short of my 15 minutes of fame.

PERFECTLY HUMBLED

One of the greatest compliments I received after the perfect game came from Don Drysdale, a Hall of Famer and 200-game winner. Obviously, with credentials like that, the guy knew baseball.

During the 1988 season, Drysdale was a radio broadcaster for the Dodgers. After my perfect game, I remember reading one of his quotes that said something like, "Tom was just putting them in the books that night. It was as easy a perfect game as you could imagine. He just shut them down."

Coming from a guy of his stature, that quote was really quite humbling. It's not every day that you get complimented like that.

I guess Drysdale really helped put things in perspective for me. Even though I'd take a Hall of Fame career or even another World Series title before a perfect game any day of the week, I did something that some of the game's greats never did. That perfect game put me in pretty unique company.

And to hear someone as prominent as Drysdale talking about how impressed he was made the whole thing that much more special.

PERFECT TIMING

One of the most satisfying aspects of the perfect game was the year I pitched it.

Danny Jackson and I both had pitched well all year, and I wanted to keep it going so we could feed off each other. That was important for us. Winning almost became contagious between the two of us.

But more importantly, I was still only a year removed from that demotion to the minor leagues.

The 1987 season was pretty much a debacle. It was the only time in my career I had a losing record with the Reds, and despite my success in 1988, I'm sure some people in the organization and even some fans maybe wondered if I would fall back into those losing ways.

By the end of 1988, I think I had put most of the fears behind everyone. And once I pitched the perfect game, I think most people had completely forgotten about the demotion.

So if you ever find yourself in the majors and really struggling, just throw a perfect game. You'd be amazed at how quickly it can smooth things over.

HIDDEN BALL TRICK

The story's been well documented over the years, but I might as well tell it again for the two of you who haven't heard it.

Yes, I kept the ball from the last out of the perfect game. But no, I have no idea where exactly it's located these days.

After that strikeout that ended the game, Jeff Reed gave me the ball, and I kept it clinched in my glove, even after I was mobbed and wrestled to the ground by my teammates.

I took it home that night and planned to keep it as a memento. I placed it on the mantle above our fireplace. It didn't have any special markings or anything else on it that said it had any type of significance.

Not long after I put it there, I noticed the ball was missing. As it turned out, the kids needed a baseball to play with. They probably didn't realize it was anything special, so I guess they just took it in the backyard to play catch. Not surprisingly, they ended up losing it in the woods behind our house.

The ball is probably still out there somewhere—with the dozens of others they've lost over the years.

HALL OF AN HONOR

Near the end of the 2004 baseball season, the Cincinnati Reds Hall of Fame and Museum opened to the public. The facility, located next door to Great American Ball Park, was built to showcase the largest collection of Reds memorabilia and artifacts anywhere in the country.

As a fan, I couldn't wait for the museum to open.

And as a former player, I couldn't wait to help out.

Greg Rhodes, the museum's executive director, contacted me to see if there were any items I'd be willing to loan for display. Obviously, my stuff would do a lot more good in the museum than in my basement, so I dropped off a small lot of items.

I handed over my replica of the 1990 World Series trophy, a jersey I wore during the 1988 season, and perhaps the most treasured piece—my glove from the perfect game.

If you're ever in Cincinnati, by all means, go check out the museum. In addition to the perfect game stuff, they have mementos tracing back all the way to the 1869 Red Stockings. It's just a great place to relive Reds history and one of the few places to catch actual video clips of the perfect game.

MRS. PERFECT'S BONUS

The day after I pitched my perfect game and Debbie got her mink coat, Marge said she also wanted to put a special clause in my contract for the next season.

Marge said she was including a clause that stated Deb would receive a $300,000 bonus if I pitched another perfect game in 1989.

I appreciated the gesture, and we all kind of got a good laugh out of the whole idea. I mean honestly, the chances of throwing one perfect game were astronomical, so the idea of pitching two seemed about as far out there as you could get.

Still, though, Marge kept the clause in my contract until the National League office made her take it out. I'm not sure of the exact reasoning behind their decision, but we weren't really too surprised.

Fast forward to the Fourth of July in 1989. We're playing in Philadelphia, and I'm taking the mound in the ninth inning with another perfect game going! I had retired 24 straight batters, and I needed just three more. I had visions of Johnny Vander Meer going through my head.

But Dickie Thon ended any bid at immortality when he doubled to lead off the inning.

Obviously, the pressure was pretty intense. But could you imagine how much worse it would have been if I had had $300,000 of my wife's money on the line?

PERFECT FANS

After all these years, a lot of people in and around Cincinnati still call me "Mr. Perfect."

I've always found it pretty funny. After all, I was only perfect for an hour and 52 minutes. Most of the other time, I was imperfect—and stubborn, immature, and even a bit of a wiseass. It doesn't matter, though. The Cincinnati fans have treated me better than I could have ever imagined despite all those faults.

For years now, the Reds have been my favorite team. Not only am I a former player, but also a lifelong fan. Etching my little spot in team lore means so much simply because it came with the Reds.

So when people around town call me Mr. Perfect, it's more humbling than you know. And I'm eternally grateful.

But that's what makes Cincinnati so great. You give the Queen City one great memory of Reds baseball, and they'll show you a lifetime of gratitude.

8

DETHRONING THE QUEEN CITY'S KING

HEADS AND TAILS

Early in spring training in 1989, Marge announced that she and Kal Daniels would settle a salary dispute with the flip of a coin. Kal wanted $325,000, but the Reds were offering $300,000.

When neither side would budge, Kal and his agent accepted Marge's offer to settle the difference by flipping a coin.

I figured it was a joke when I first heard about it, but it turned out to be legit, and it quickly became big news. Some of the TV stations even covered it live from the parking lot at our spring-training complex.

One flip of the coin later, and Kal was $25,000 richer. He literally beat Marge at her own game.

I couldn't help playing devil's advocate. Could you imagine the backlash if Kal had lost? Could you imagine the field day the media would have had? But maybe that was Marge's goal all along.

Marge had funny ways of going about things sometimes. Proposing the coin flip wasn't usually the way she handled her business. After all, when it came to contract negotiations, she could be one of the toughest broads I know.

Instead, Marge was probably just looking for a way to have some fun and kick off the season in an interesting way. And, it seemed to work. Everyone got a good laugh (except for the commissioner's office, which warned Marge that similar "negotiations" would result in stiff penalties).

Unfortunately, the coin flip was one of the few bright spots in 1989.

A few weeks later, we learned that our world—and Pete's—was about to turn upside down.

PETE'S MEETING

It was a few weeks into spring training 1989 that we learned Pete had been asked to go to New York to meet with commissioner Peter Ueberroth and commissioner-elect Bart Giammati. Soon after, they made an announcement that Pete was being investigated for "serious" allegations.

There were a lot of rumors going around, but no one in the clubhouse really knew what it was about.

Regardless, Pete called a meeting to say that whatever was going on wouldn't affect us or find its way into the clubhouse. He told us just to concentrate on getting ready for the season and ignore everything else going on.

Obviously, the media flocked to our spring training, but just as Pete promised, he didn't really let the circus find its way to us.

I think the majority of the guys didn't think it had anything to do with gambling on baseball. At the time, a lot of the guys went to the track and bet on football and basketball games, and Pete was no different. If anything, we thought maybe it had to do with that type of gambling, or maybe something like an outstanding gambling debt that the commissioner's office heard about.

Back then, Pete had a lot of cronies like Paul Janzen and Tommy Gioiosa hanging around him. We called them "green flies"—guys who hung around for the scraps. But even though they seemed to be around all the time, they were never really a distraction to us, so we pretty much ignored them.

Besides, everyone entered the 1989 season with pretty big hopes. We had four straight second-place finishes under Pete, and we really thought it would be the year we got over the hump and make the postseason.

The investigation stayed in the back of our minds for most of the season, but we didn't dwell on it. Pete made sure of that. At least initially, our focus was on the coming season.

COLD FEET

One day during that spring, Norm Charlton came into the clubhouse and found a surprise by his locker.

Scott Scudder had taken Norm's cleats and placed them in a bucket of water—and then froze them solid. The spikes were perfectly preserved in a big chunk of ice.

We all got a good laugh out of it, and surprisingly, Norm was a pretty good sport about it.

That's not to say he didn't get his revenge, though.

When Scudder left for his afternoon workout, Norm decided to up the ante.

Scudder returned from the field later that day. After he showered and got dressed, he went out to the parking lot.

He found his car sitting on blocks.

Norm came out to the parking lot laughing his butt off. Scudder let Norm go on for a while. After all, he was pretty much asking for some type of retaliation, and all things considered, Scudder probably figured he got off pretty easy.

After a minute or two, his facial expression completely changed.

"Uh, Norm, where exactly *are* my tires?" he asked.

Norm didn't say a word. He just pointed to the roof for the second part of his prank.

I have no idea how he got up there, but Norm had neatly arranged all four tires on the top of the spring-training complex.

PLANE STUPIDITY

One of the perks of playing in the pros was traveling by charter. It was as comfy a plane as you could imagine, with all the munchies you could ever want. It also had adult beverages, if you were so inclined. And we were plenty inclined.

One time we were heading back from Houston and wanted to play cards, but there was no good way to make a table for all of us. We had a few too many cocktails in us, and we were generally acting like idiots. So we tore off some of the fold-down trays and made a makeshift table of our own.

I think just about everyone got a little destructive on that flight, and soon, it looked like a tornado had ripped through the plane.

Not long after, Marge Schott heard about what we did, and she received a pretty big repair bill for all the destruction.

Marge hated coming down on us. She really wanted to be liked by the players, and I think she got a little intimidated when she had to be the disciplinarian. But this time, we had gone too far.

To get her point across, Marge made us fly commercially for a while. Here we are, a professional ball club, flying coach just like everyone else. It was a pretty humbling experience.

And Marge got her point across: If we were going to act like children, she was going to treat us like children.

PAUL'S PUNT

There was only one time I ever remember losing a game and having a smile on my face afterward.

It happened at Philadelphia in 1989. The score was tied in the 10th inning, and Lenny Dykstra was up to bat for the Phillies. Lenny lined a shot to right field while Steve Jeltz, a runner on second, made a dash toward third.

Paul O'Neill charged for the ball hoping to nail Jeltz at home, but the ball dropped in front of him. He reached down to pick it up, but he bobbled it. And then he bobbled it again. And as the ball hit the turf again, Paul just kicked the ball out of sheer frustration, thinking Jeltz was already headed to home to score easily.

But the kick was an absolute perfect punt to Todd Benzinger at first.

And as it turned out, Jeltz stumbled around third base. When he saw Paul's dead-on kick, he had to hold up and never made it around to score.

At first, no one could really believe what had happened. Paul was the ultimate competitor, so he was still fuming that he hadn't gotten to the ball on the first try. But we quickly realized that the runner never scored only because that kick was so accurate. A few feet in either direction, and the ballgame would have been over right then.

Unfortunately, the Phils ended up scoring on a passed ball soon after that and won the game.

But it was one of the few losses we actually got a kick out of.

FUNNY BONES

Right before the start of the 1989 season, the Reds signed Kent Tekulve to a contract. "Teek" was a skinny journeyman reliever with 15 seasons under his belt.

And believe it or not, I think he wore the same suit every one of those seasons.

That road outfit was just awful. He had some type of tweed jacket with green and yellow and every other color you could imagine mixed in. He completed the outfit with a pair of white shoes that he had to polish before every trip.

Although Teek had been pitching since the early 1970s, I couldn't imagine that getup ever being in style.

Teek started off the season well with us, but he had a rough June and July, and he was soon having a tough time getting batters out.

One day he walked into the clubhouse and announced he was finished. He was retiring, and his mind was made up.

It was obvious he had given his decision a lot of thought, so we knew better than trying to talk him out of it. Besides, at 42, he was no spring chicken.

Once we received word of his retirement, we knew we had to do something to send him out in style. He had entertained us all season with stories from his career, and we really looked up to the guy.

At the time, Teek was about six and a half feet tall and weighed maybe 180 pounds.

So we took the skeleton out of the trainer's room and put a Reds hat on it. We then taped a little cigarette to its mouth. If we could have found a pair of tinted glasses and an ugly suit coat, it would have been like he never left.

We put the skeleton right next to Teek's locker, and when he returned to the clubhouse, he cracked up at the sight of his twin.

"Looks just like you, huh?" I joked.

Teek thanked us all for our hospitality that season, and he said he was going to miss the clubhouse camaraderie more than anything.

Teek was a true professional—no bones about it.

LEERY OF LEARY

Like I've said before, I hit very few guys on purpose during my career. I sent my fair share of warning pitches, though, and every once in a while I'd have to answer for them.

In July, the Reds traded Kal Daniels and Lenny Harris to the Dodgers for Mariano Duncan and Tim Leary.

"Tim Leary? Yikes," I thought.

Earlier that season, I had faced Leary and the Dodgers, and he had gotten a couple hits off me. Every pitcher hates giving up hits to other pitchers. It's just embarrassing. So the next time Leary came to the plate, I threw one behind his head. I didn't hit him, but I didn't want him feeling comfortable up there. I got a dirty look, but no punches were thrown.

Well, the day after the trade, I was fumbling around my locker at Riverfront when I heard a strange voice.

"Well, if it isn't the guy who tried to take my head off," he said.

I knew right away who it was.

"What'd you expect?" I said, never turning around. "I can't let some hack pitcher get three hits off me."

I half expected a baseball to come flying at me, but instead, I just heard some laughing. So I turned around and shook hands with my new teammate.

Thank God the guy had a sense of humor.

HOUSTON HAS A PROBLEM

Jim Kaat, my pitching coach in 1985, used to joke that every pitcher should enter the first inning hoping to make the first two outs when his team is batting. In other words, he wants the other eight guys in the lineup to bat twice without making an out. It's a pretty lofty goal, and amazingly, it almost happened in August 1989.

We were playing the Astros, and we exploded for 14 runs in the first inning.

Eight straight guys made it on base, and then I grounded out. But on the second time through the lineup, everyone got a hit, even me.

We sent every guy to the plate twice (18 batters!), and we had only one out.

The next two guys flied out, though, and then I entered the top of the second with a 14-0 lead.

Someone once asked me how you pitch with a lead like that.

"Well, you sure as hell don't walk anyone," I said.

And I didn't. Instead, Glenn Davis led off the next inning with a home run.

But the rest of the damage was pretty minimal. I threw a complete game and got the win in the eventual 18-2 victory.

They say you see something new every day, and that day, I was just happy to be on the good end of it.

We set all kinds of records that day, and every single starter got at least a hit. Seven of the guys got at least two hits. And Rolando Roomes, Todd Benzinger, and Jeff Reed all had three hits.

But the most amazing stat of the day? Time of game: 2:16.

TAKING 10 FOR THE TEAM

During that 18-2 rout of the Astros, I did see one really classy move.

Obviously, the Houston pitchers were getting pounded that day. Starter Jim Clancy left the game without recording a single out, and then veteran Bob Forsch came in for mop-up duty.

But Forsch got pounded, too.

At one point in the first inning, I heard they were going to take him out of the game.

"Look, the game's already out of hand," he said. "Just keep me in here. Save the bullpen. I'll do what I can."

Talk about a team-first mentality.

No pitcher likes getting his brains beat in like that. It bruises your ego—and your ERA. But Bob had been around the game long enough to know that no good would come from burning up the rest of the bullpen, especially when the game that was so far out of reach.

Bob ended up surrendering 18 hits and 10 earned runs, but he pitched seven much-needed innings for the Astros.

It was an ugly stat line, but it came from one of the classiest moves I can remember.

WHEN CHARLIE GOT HUSTLED

At the end of August that year, we headed home after sweeping the Cubs in Chicago.

We had an off-day scheduled, so I went home to spend some time with the family.

I was lounging around the house and watching TV when they broke in with a news report.

"Reds Manager Pete Rose Banned from Baseball," flashed on the screen.

I sat there, completely stunned. I couldn't believe what I was seeing—my leader and hero plastered on the news channels, saying he had been kicked out of baseball.

I didn't even know what to think. It just didn't feel right.

At first, they said Pete signed a confession saying he placed bets with bookmakers and consorted with felons, which were both offenses serious enough to have him permanently banned. But as part of the agreement for that confession, Pete was told he could apply for reinstatement after one year, and there would be no formal findings that tied Pete to betting on baseball or the Reds.

I was glued to the TV, trying to make sense of it all.

"OK," I thought, "it sounds like he'll be back in a year. He'll get past this. We'll move on."

Soon after, though, commissioner Bart Giamatti came on TV and said that he had personally concluded that Pete did, in fact, bet on baseball.

It was total bush league! No matter what actually happened, they had an agreement, and Giamatti completely ignored it. He totally sold Pete out.

Obviously, Pete would have never agreed to the conditions if he knew he was going to be barbequed like that.

PETE'S BEAT

I returned to Riverfront Stadium the next day to a clubhouse in total shock and disbelief. We knew Pete wasn't running with the best crowd, but none of us could have imagined the extent of it.

No one really talked in much detail about it. It was a pretty somber environment.

It was just too far out there for any of us to make sense of it. We all just wanted to hear what Pete had to say, but he was gone for good.

Pete initially denied all the charges. In fact, he denied it for more than 15 years afterward.

And probably naïvely, I was one of the guys who believed him.

After seeing Giamatti completely screw him over like that, it was easy to feel that Pete was getting shafted from the start. If Giamatti was willing to blow off an agreement the same day he signed it, who was to say he wasn't willing to set Pete up?

Unfortunately, eight days after the announcement of Pete's ban from baseball, Giamatti died of a heart attack.

I'm sure the stress of the situation played a part in his death, although Giamatti was a known smoker and carried around a lot of weight.

It was just a tragic ending to a terrible week.

It was also a dark day in Cincinnati and all of Major League Baseball. And for all we knew, any chance of Pete's reinstatement or a justification for Giamatti's actions expired with the commissioner.

I knew that things would never be the same. The only major league manager I had ever known—the only manager that most of our roster had ever known—was gone from baseball.

MORE THOUGHTS ON PETE

From everything I've watched and read since Pete's banishment from baseball, it appears he never bet against the Reds.

I suppose that says something about his personality. He believed in his team so much, he expected them to win every night. After all, that's what Pete was paid to do—win. And for the most part, that's exactly what he did. We hadn't won the big one, but we were contenders every season with him as our manager.

Some people claim that Pete put us all at risk by betting on his own team. They said he probably left pitchers in too long, overworked the regulars, and generally took a gamble with his players' health.

Let me be clear: I never, ever saw any of that.

Pete was intense and he demanded 110 percent every day, but he would never do anything to put us in danger. I can't remember a single instance on the field that made me think he didn't care about our health. There were no weird substitutions, no taxing the bullpen for unapparent reasons, no questionable tactics of any kind.

Pete and I share a dugout one final time during his softball game at Cinergy Field in 2002.
Photo courtesy of the Cincinnati Reds

However, that's not to say I thought Pete's behavior was acceptable. What he did was wrong. Very wrong. He permanently stained the game. He ruined his career. And he did a huge injustice to the fans of Cincinnati.

But to compare him to the 1919 Chicago White Sox is just wrong. Those guys took money to guarantee a loss. The Black Sox teamed up with gangsters to assure an outcome of a game.

We're talking about two very different situations, but people want to lump them together. Personally, I feel like it's trying to compare apples and oranges.

Unfortunately, the commissioner's office was quick to group them together, probably because of the embarrassment he brought to baseball.

Pete paid a heavy price not just because of what he did, but also because he was able to get away with it for so long. He skirted the system for years, and they were determined to make him pay the price.

HINDSIGHT MAKES THINGS CLEARER

Back in 1988, I was watching TV with Pete in the clubhouse lounge. We were getting ready for an afternoon game, and we started talking about the Giants–Padres game from the night before.

Eric Show had been starting for the Padres and had given up some runs late in the game to blow the lead. They had some guys warming up in the bullpen, and I just couldn't understand why they had left him in the game.

"What were they thinking?" I asked. "They should have pulled him."

For some reason, that really set off Pete.

"What, are you a manager now?" he asked me. "What do you care who wins? What the hell do you know anyway?"

The attack was vicious and seemed kind of personal. At the time, it really made no sense. For a year afterward, that whole exchange stuck with me.

Looking back, I think I now know what caused the outburst: Pete probably had money on the game.

When I questioned the decision to leave in Show, he probably felt like I was rooting against the Giants, the team Pete bet on to win.

When the news came down that Pete was banned for betting on baseball, the whole situation made a little more sense.

I was looking at the situation like a player, not a gambler. It didn't matter to me who won the stupid game. I just wondered why they didn't go to the bullpen in a situation like that.

Pete, though, likely had something riding on the outcome of that game. The situation just would have made a lot more sense if I had known it at the time.

TOMMY'S TROUBLES

After Pete was banned, the Reds named Tommy Helms the interim manager. Tommy had been one of Pete's coaches, and he knew the team better than anyone.

But he never stood a chance.

Tommy was considered one of "Pete's guys," and I think people felt he was tainted or somehow associated with the whole gambling mess. There was (and still is), of course, no proof of that, but people seemed to believe it anyway.

Not surprisingly, the team soon fell apart under Tommy. We went 5-14 to close out the season, dropping to 75-87 and fifth place in the standings.

And the team became a mess.

A perfect example came late in the season when we were playing in Atlanta. Rob Dibble came to bat in the eighth with the bases loaded. On a 2-0 pitch, he was ordered to take a pitch. He ignored it, though, and promptly flied out.

Tommy was so ticked, he told "Dibs" to pack up his stuff and go home because his season was over.

The official reasoning was insubordination, but that was just a fancy way of saying that Dibs had his head up his ass. There was no reason to swing at a pitch in that situation, especially with no outs in the inning. Besides, Dibble didn't have a hit his entire career. No one knew what he was thinking.

By that time, though, the inmates were running the asylum. Neither Tommy nor anyone else in that situation could have made the rest of that season anything but a disaster.

With Pete gone, the team's legs were cut out from underneath us.

And for the first time in a long time, I wasn't going to miss baseball. I just wanted to go home and put the entire 1989 season behind me.

9

WIRE-TO-WIRE CHAMPS

LOU, MEET PETE

Prior to the 1990 season, the Reds hired Lou Piniella to take over the reins of the club.

Lou had managed the Yankees for a time, but after a rocky relationship with owner George Steinbrenner, he headed to Cincinnati to manage our club, probably at the urging of our general manager Bob Quinn, another Yankees refugee.

Bob must have known Lou was going to have his work cut out for him. In essence, he was replacing Pete Rose, a legend in Cincinnati.

However, because of a month-long lockout to start the season, Lou would have to wait a while to meet his new team.

One day during the lockout, Pete invited me to play golf with him at Walden Lake Golf Course in Plant City. Pete had a place down in Tampa, and because of the lockout, I had some free time, so I was happy to accept his invitation.

We were on the eighth hole, which was tucked behind some palmetto trees and ran along a local road. Lou must have noticed me while he was driving by. We had never met, but I'm sure he was itching to meet some of his players, so he pulled over and walked about 30 yards to our tee box.

Lou, though, hadn't noticed that Pete was with me.

We were shaking hands before he looked over and saw Pete standing there.

It was a tense—and intense—moment. I wasn't sure if I should even introduce them. After all, Lou was here pretty much to take over Pete's team, one that Pete spent four seasons putting together and slowly turning into a winner. Then, it had been taken away when Pete was kicked out of baseball. And now it was handed over to this new guy.

Luckily, Lou got me off the hot seat.

"Pete, I'm Lou Piniella, and it's a pleasure to meet you," he said, offering a handshake. "If you wouldn't mind some time, I'd really like to sit down and talk to you about *your* team."

It was amazing how quickly any tension I felt completely went away. Lou couldn't have possibly said anything better to diffuse the situation. He acknowledged that it was, in fact, Pete's team, which I'm sure made our former skipper happy.

I knew right then we had something special in Lou.

LITTLE BIG LEAGUE

Because of the lockout, we were kind of on our own to get ready for the season. For some guys, that meant trips to Disney World with the family. Most guys, though, got together for our own practices.

Guys like Eric Davis, Barry Larkin, and Rick Mahler would assemble the troops, and we'd head to any open fields we could find. Because of the lockout, we had no access to our regular spring-training facilities, so Plant City High School and even Little League fields became our makeshift headquarters. We did all the normal stuff—hit fungos, worked on relay throws, and threw from the mound to get our legs back underneath us. All of the usual spring rituals.

But looking back, I guess it's kind of funny. Here we were, the eventual World Series champions, hoping a tee ball or softball team didn't kick us off their field.

READY TO WIN

Ask any guy who was in the clubhouse for our first meeting, and he'll remember Lou's speech like it was yesterday.

We'd soon learn that Lou didn't pull any punches, and he sure as hell didn't mince words. Spring training got a late start because of the lockout, and he was ready to get down to business.

"Look, you guys are way too talented not to win," he said. "You're here to win, and I'm here to win. And I don't give a damn if you don't like me."

That was it.

If nothing else, you had to respect Lou's bluntness.

His speech, though, set the stage for our season. No matter what distractions, differences, or problems we might have, there was one thing we all shared, and that was a desire to win.

BERNIE'S CLUBHOUSE

One of the greatest jokesters in the Reds locker room wasn't a player, manager, or coach. He was the clubhouse manager, and he probably had the most sadistic sense of humor of anyone in baseball.

But you had to love Bernie Stowe.

The guy started off as a batboy back in 1947 and has worked in the clubhouse ever since. Like Joe Nuxhall, he's a true throwback, with almost 60 years of service time under his belt.

Bernie, though, was one of those silent mischievous types. Unsuspecting rookies never saw it coming.

He used to keep a little cage in his work area. It was cluttered up with stuff, and all you could see were some newspaper scraps and a clump of hair.

"Hey, rook," he'd say, "come see my mongoose."

Once he had a gullible newbie peaking in the cage, Bernie would hit a button that shot open a door and fired out a hairy blob. Grown men would shriek like little girls and scramble for the nearest exit. It was classic.

Other times, when spring training was winding down and cut days were approaching, Bernie would walk by the lockers of likely casualties while sporting an invisible machine gun. He'd gun down the locker, making shooting sounds and shaking his upper body like he was Rambo, before walking away with an evil grin on his face. The guy was merciless.

But my favorite gag came with a homemade touch. Bernie was the guy who stitched uniform numbers and players' names on our jerseys, so he was no stranger to needle and thread. Some days, he'd walk around covered in an apron, as though he had just finished preparing our lunch or dinner spread. But then he'd flip up the apron and flash you a hand-stitched set of male genitalia made out of a stuffed sock.

And based on its circus-like size, it was obvious Bernie thought very highly of himself.

OPENING MARKS

Our nemesis—or least my nemesis—during the 1990 season was Houston. Although my college buddy Jimmy Deshaies was on their team, I just despised the Astros.

During our shortened camp, I somehow ended up facing Houston three or four times that spring. And Glenn Davis, one of their studs, hit a home run every game. I ended up throwing outside or over the plate every time, and he crushed one each time.

So when we opened the season in Houston (the lockout screwed up the schedule and kept us from opening at home) and I was given the Opening Day start, I vowed I wouldn't make the same mistake again. When Davis came to bat, he was nearly standing on the plate. I threw inside anyway, and he got hit. The next time up, he stood on the plate again, so he got hit again.

The Astros felt like it was intentional. They were furious and complained to the National League office—on the same exact day they hit Barry Larkin and nearly took off Eric Davis's head. Apparently, the Astros had short memories.

Unfortunately for them, all Houston did was light a spark under us. We rallied together and soon kicked off the season in record fashion.

WIRE TO WIRE

After a sweep of the Astros in that heated opening series, we continued to win—often and easily.

We won nine straight games to open the season, which was a new club record. But it didn't stop there. At one point, our record stood at 30-12, and we had built a sizeable cushion in the standings.

As it turned out, we led in the standings every day of the 1990 season. The Dodgers got within a few games at one point, but they never caught us.

Perhaps Lou was right—we were too talented not to win.

We became the first team in National League history to lead the division from beginning to end. In Reds history, we secured our unique spot as the wire-to-wire champs. Not even the Big Red Machine could stake claim to that.

I think everyone sensed pretty early on that we were destined for something special. From the first month in the season, Randy Myers kept a chart in his locker. It counted down our march toward 99 wins and a division championship.

At first, Randy's chart seemed a little premature. But we kept reeling off wins, and Randy ready kept ticking off more and more victories.

When times were good, I loved looking at that thing. It showed us how far we had come and how much we accomplished. But when times were bad and the wins were few and far between, it just showed us how much we had to lose.

THE NASTY BOYS

Back in 1990, there was a TV show about undercover cops working for the Las Vegas Police Department called *Nasty Boys*.

Soon, our bullpen trio of Norm Charlton, Rob Dibble, and Randy Myers adopted the name, and it took off, getting bigger and bigger as the season went on. Soon, they had T-shirts made, and a guy from Texas even sent them "Nasty Boys" cowboy boots with their names stitched on them.

However, the name could've just as well originated from their spring-training diet. The three of them would send out clubhouse assistants to pick up McDonald's. They'd eat that crap every day. While the rest of us got by on a menu of soups and salads, they feasted almost exclusively on those disgusting Big Macs and quarter-pounders.

However, that was about the only thing they had in common. The group was one of the oddest collections of characters you could imagine.

Norm was the brains of the group, a triple major from Rice University who loved the outdoors. The lefty threw a nasty forkball that made him almost unhittable to left-handed hitters.

Dibs was the brawn of the operation, and he was easily the most intimidating pitcher of his time. He could throw 100 miles per hour, and he backed down from no one.

And as I liked to joke, Randy was just the closer who reaped the benefits of the other two.

Seriously, though, Randy was a bit of a wild card, too. He liked to portray himself as a soldier of fortune. He wore military fatigues under his uniform and kept disarmed hand grenades and knives in his locker. His spot in the clubhouse soon looked like an Army surplus store.

Together, they formed the most dominating bullpen I had ever seen, and they were a vital part in our march toward the postseason.

CRACK-SCHOTT

Marge was a shrewd businesswoman. Although she kept Reds games and concessions affordable for fans, she wasn't above any gimmick or oddball sales tactic, even when it came to our discarded equipment.

She used to order batboys to collect all cracked bats that were no longer in use. She'd then put them up for sale in the Reds' team store and market them as "game-used" bats, and I'm sure she made a tidy profit.

Once the players caught word of her new venture, we tried to cut off the supply. Once a bat was cracked, we'd bang it against or wall or jump on it to break it into more than one piece.

As we figured, "game-used" was a lot more valuable than "split-in-two."

(Coauthor's note: The tradition lived for years after the 1990 team. When we packed up the Reds offices to move from Cinergy Field to Great American Ball Park, we found literally thousands of broken bats in storage. Dennys Reyes, a pitcher with just 29 career at-bats in Cincinnati, had somehow accumulated a lot of nearly 30 bats that were broken into two. Yet, a "cracked" bat was nowhere to be found.)

STANLEY STEAMER, PITCHER BEANER

Our pitching coach in 1990 was Stan Williams. He used to be a Dodger with Don Drysdale. Like him, Stan was fearless on the mound, even after he retired and became a coach.

Stan was better known as "Steamer," which was probably a tribute to his fastball, though it was also a fitting description of his personality.

Steamer once told us about a clause in his contract that called for a $10,000 bonus if he walked fewer than 100 batters.

"Once I got to 90 walks that season, I had a new game plan," he told us. "If the count went to three balls on a batter, I'd just hit the bastard."

When he took over coaching duties for the Reds, he used to throw batting practice to the pitchers. If you had the audacity to hit a home run or knock one up the middle at him, Steamer would throw the next pitch right at your chin.

We thought the guy was nuts.

We had a ton of giants on that team—Rob Dibble, Ron Robinson, and Tim Birtsas, to name a few—but no one dared charge the mound. Even at 54, Steamer could probably still kick all our butts. The bravest we usually got was "unintentionally" losing our grip during a swing and flinging a bat in Steamer's direction.

He'd usually just smile—and then throw one at our head.

RACE RELATIONS

The greatest thing about our squad in 1990 was the unity. We didn't see whites or blacks or Hispanics. We just saw each other as ballplayers and teammates. We'd all go out together, and everyone got along. It was the closest-knit team I've ever been a part of.

Early in the season, we traded Mike Roesler and Jeff Richardson to Pittsburgh for a speedy outfielder named Billy Hatcher.

Ronnie Oester knew that Hatcher had played with Buddy Bell in Houston, so he called him to find out more about our new teammate.

"He's a good kid," Buddy told him. "He works hard and has a great sense of humor. He'll fit in just fine with you guys."

The next day, Hatcher came walking into our clubhouse. I'm sure he was a little nervous, wondering how his teammates would welcome him to Cincinnati.

Right then, Ronnie yelled from the back of the clubhouse.

"Hey! Who's the new colored boy?"

In probably any other clubhouse, a race war would have broken out. Ours was different, though. We could joke about even the touchiest of subjects.

Hatcher had obviously been warned about our team's warped sense of humor. He just started laughing and introduced himself to all of us.

And Buddy was right; he fit right in.

THE WRONG SCUFF

I only tried throwing a doctored ball once in my career. And it wasn't even mine. Nor did it do me much good.

We were playing the Houston Astros in the Astrodome. Back then, Houston pitchers were known for throwing a doctored ball every now and then, and this night was no different.

I don't want to name names, but let's just say that the guilty party had won just two games all year and his strikeout totals had dropped noticeably that season. So when his fastball all the sudden came to life again against us, we knew the reason.

My suspicions were confirmed when I went to take the mound in the fourth inning. I picked up the ball and noticed a big cut.

Once I came back to the dugout, Lou pulled me aside.

"Was that ball scuffed?" he asked.

"Sure was."

"Why didn't you use it?"

"I did! But I had no idea where the damn thing was going once I threw it."

"Well, why in the hell didn't you throw it over to me?"

I looked down, and Lou had amassed a pile of about a dozen doctored balls. He kind of looked like a mother bird protecting its nest. It was his stockpile of evidence.

Lou ended up complaining to the umpires, but even with evidence, the Astros were never confronted. Obviously, though, Houston realized that we knew what was going on. And their strikeouts stopped almost immediately.

And it was no big secret why.

OESTERDOME

When you're losing, you'll try anything to shake out of a slump.

Ronnie Oester proved it in July.

We had just lost a game to the Dodgers, and it was our eighth loss in a row. Lou was steaming. He came into the clubhouse and was kicking everything and screaming before he went into his office and slammed the door.

We were still in first place, but the Dodgers kept getting closer and closer to us in the standings. After Lou went off, everyone just kind of sat there and looked beaten.

Ronnie then called out Rob Dibble and Norm Charlton, who had talked about shaving their heads a few days earlier in hopes they'd break out of the losing streak. For some reason, shaving your head always seems to be a last resort for teams stuck in a skid.

Dibs and Charlton backpedaled, though, saying they'd shave their heads only if they lost 10 in a row.

"Ten games? Ten games? Why would you want us to lose even more games? That's so stupid!" Ronnie yelled.

So Ronnie told Eric Davis to grab his clippers and buzz him. I think he thought everyone else would join him, but Ronnie was the only one brave enough to do it.

I guess it worked, though. We won the next night.

But if you see Ronnie nowadays, you'll notice that his hair never did grow back.

HOTHEADED

I was pitching in Atlanta one time. I had given up some runs, and Lou soon took me out of the game. We were leading, but I was pretty ticked. I never liked being pulled early. I always thought I could keep us in a ballgame if I was given the chance. But I knew better than to argue with Lou.

Not long after, the Braves tied the game, so there was no way I would get the win.

I grabbed a bat, and I started beating it against a wall in frustration. I was yelling obscenities with each swing, but I instantly stopped when I saw Lou looking at me. I fully expected him to yell at me for acting like an idiot. Instead, he just threw some fuel on the fire.

"Yeah, well, I'd be pissed, too, if I were pitching like you."

THE BAT DOCTOR

Tony Perez was a coach in 1990, and you could always count on him to lighten the mood in the dugout and clubhouse.

"Doggy" wasn't exactly the sympathetic type, though. Lord help the guy who struck out and came back to the bench looking for some words of encouragement. Instead, Doggy would go, "Ewww, yuck!" before sliding down the bench as though striking out was some sort of contagious disease. It was hard to be too upset when you had a 48-year-old grown man acting like you had cooties.

And if you ever broke a bat, Doggy was on the case. Snap a bat in two, and you'd usually find it in your locker the next day covered in Band-Aids and trainers tape.

A NASTY REALITY

The regulars in the 1990 starting rotation were Jose Rijo, Danny Jackson, Jack Armstrong, and me. Rick Mahler had some starts early in the season, and Norm Charlton had some down the stretch.

We were a solid bunch. But we had to be. Otherwise, Lou didn't think twice about pulling us early in the game.

That was the price we paid for having the Nasty Boys in the bullpen. Although it was good to know you had those guys waiting in the wings to conserve your leads, it also meant that you were going to get an early hook at the first sign of trouble.

We felt like we needed to have a no-hitter or at least a shutout going if we wanted to pitch late into a game.

Combined the Nasty Boys went 24-18 with a 2.32 ERA and 351 strikeouts in 334 innings pitched in 1990, so it was hard to argue with Lou's philosophy.

They were nasty, all right—to opposing hitters, as well as to their own starting pitchers.

NO PLACE LIKE HOME

I can't recall a single time during the 1990 season that I didn't look forward to going to the clubhouse. Every day I couldn't wait to get to the stadium to see all the guys.

Usually by the end of a season, you can't stand looking at most of your teammates. It's not that you hate them. It's just that after a month and a half of spring training and six months of the regular season almost every day, you're just ready for some time apart—especially if you're losing.

In 1990, however, it was just a fun place to be. The clubhouse was always rocking—loud music, lots of joking around, and just a ton of guys that were fun to hang out with.

That season, I just couldn't think of a place I'd rather be.

HOLLYWOOD REDS

One time while we were playing in Atlanta in 1990, I was introduced to Charlie Sheen, an actor who had been in a number of TV shows and movies, including one of my favorites, *Major League*.

As it turned out, Charlie, who's a native of Dayton, Ohio, was a huge Reds fan. Although he was living in Los Angeles, he said he still followed the Reds religiously. So I told him to give me a call the next time we were in L.A. so we could bring him to the park.

There's kind of this bond between actors and athletes. All of us want to be actors, and all of the actors want to be ballplayers. So the next time we were in L.A., he gave me a call.

We got Charlie a uniform and let him take batting practice with us, and later that night, we hung out at the hotel bar. To thank us for our generosity, Charlie said he wanted to throw us a party at his place the next time we were in town.

"There's just one condition," I told him. "It's got to be on the night I pitch. That's the only night I go out, and there's no way I'm missing the party."

So Charlie made the arrangements. Once we got there, he gave us a tour of the place, and as he opened a door to his backyard, the fog came rolling into his house. Charlie lived in the mountains around Malibu, so his place was so cool. He had purchased a lot of baseball memorabilia from auctions and collectors, and he had his house filled with all kinds of stuff, including a Ted Williams autographed baseball, a Babe Ruth bat, and even a ball from the night of my perfect game.

I kept in touch with Charlie in the months afterward, and the next year, he said he wanted to have another party for us.

"Again, the same condition," I told him. "It's gotta be on the night I pitch."

We had one other condition that year, too: No coaches allowed. I wanted the guys to be able to enjoy themselves, and that's hard to do if you think someone is always looking over your shoulder.

I arranged for the limos to pick up all of the players right from Dodger Stadium.

Once we got to Charlie's, I noticed that the party was definitely a little bigger the second time around. People were everywhere. The place was packed.

I found a place to sit down and talk to Charlie. He then introduced me to a friend of his named Heidi. The three of us talked for about an hour, and she seemed nice enough. But I left without learning much more about her.

All of the guys had a good time that night, and it was probably 8 a.m. before the final limo left.

Not long after the party, I was watching the nightly news and saw a familiar face on the screen. I soon realized it was Charlie's friend Heidi. But they were calling her something else: "Hollywood Madam" Heidi Fleiss.

Little did I know I had been talking to such a Tinseltown legend that night.

A FAIR SHARE

In August, the Reds released Ken Griffey Sr., one of the few real veterans of our club.

It was believed that team management wanted to open some roster spots before September call-ups, and they had asked Griffey to go on the disabled list to accommodate the new guys. When Griffey pointed out that he wasn't actually injured and therefore couldn't go on the disabled list, he was released instead.

The guys in the clubhouse weren't too thrilled about the move, but we made sure he got a fair shake when it came time to dish out World Series shares.

Once you make it to the Series, you get a pool of extra money from the additional ticket sales and broadcasting revenue to split among the players. The players vote on how much each guy gets, so you can give full or partial shares depending on how long each person was with the team.

Feeling Griffey was penalized for his honesty, we voted almost unanimously to give him a full share. It only seemed fair.

LOU LOSES IT

By the end of August, we were stuck in a skid. We had lost five straight, our offense was nonexistent, and the Dodgers were inching closer and closer in the standings.

Desperate times call for desperate measures, I suppose.

We were hosting the Cubs, and the bases were loaded in the sixth inning. Barry Larkin hit a grounder to short, and Domingo Ramos flipped to Ryne Sandberg in hopes of a double play. Sandberg fired to first, but Larkin looked like he beat the throw.

First-base umpire Dutch Rennert didn't agree, though, and he called Larkin out.

Lou instantly stormed onto the field. He ripped off his hat and fired it at Dutch's feet, which earned him a quick ejection.

But that was just the beginning. Lou was far from finished.

He then pulled first base out of the ground and using both hands, heaved it toward the outfield. I couldn't believe what I was seeing. Lou had finally lost it, I thought. We had finally pushed him over the edge.

And the show went on.

Apparently embarrassed by his first throw (which, I must admit, was rather pathetic), Lou picked up the base and heaved it again—this time with a little more "umph."

Lou nearly fell right on his keister with that throw. His face was bright red, he was screaming, and spit was flying out of his mouth while he stomped around the field. I didn't know whether to laugh or run for cover. The fans, though, loved it and continued to egg him on.

That was Lou, though. He could go off at a snap. It was probably that Latin blood in him. Even in his playing days, he had a legendary temper.

I'll never know if Lou was really that mad about the call, or if he was just trying to do something to shake us out of our losing skid.

Either way, we won six out of our next seven games at a time we needed it the most. And Lou provided us an unforgettable memory from the 1990 season.

TOO NASTY

Statistically, our team didn't really have a major leader. Everyone did a little of something, and together, it was just enough to win us a title.

But one guy we all seemed to rally around was Barry Larkin. It was Barry's fifth season in the league, and he was quickly emerging as one of the game's best offensive and defensive shortstops. When Lark struggled, we all seemed to struggle. But when he was streaking, we couldn't seem to lose.

So when one of our own guys needlessly put Lark at risk, Ronnie Oester had to step in and say something.

It was late in the season, and we were in Houston. For no apparent reason, Rob Dibble threw a pitch at Houston's shortstop, Rafael Ramirez. It seemed totally unprovoked, and in the context of the game, it just didn't make any sense.

The Astros soon retaliated and hit Lark, and at first, it looked like it might have done some serious damage.

After the game, Ronnie heard Dibble talking to Randy Myers in the clubhouse.

"That's great," said Dibs. "Now they're gonna blame me for Lark getting injured."

Ronnie overheard him and knew he had to say something.

"Of course, we're gonna blame you!" Ronnie yelled. "Lark's the catalyst of this team! If we're going to make it in the postseason, we need him healthy!"

As much as Ronnie loved Dibs, he sometimes had to be kept in check.

That's what veteran leaders like Ronnie had to do. He had to make sure everyone had his eyes on what was really important. And that wasn't going to happen with our best player on the disabled list.

QUIETLY CLINCHED

I had thought all season about what it would be like when we finally clinched the division. After a string of second-place finishes, I couldn't wait to experience it for the first time.

Unfortunately, it came in fairly unremarkable fashion. We were actually sitting in the clubhouse, waiting out a rain delay, when we learned that the Dodgers had lost and officially knocked themselves out of the race.

Honestly, we knew it was only a matter of time. We had built up a good lead in the standings, and it would have taken a miracle for L.A. to catch us during that last week. So what we felt wasn't so much enthusiasm as relief.

Once they announced we clinched, I looked to the guy in the locker next to me. It was Billy Doran, a guy who came over from Houston in August. We shook hands and congratulated each other. There were still fans in the stadium waiting out the rain delay, so some of our guys went out to the field to celebrate with them.

It was the first time I had ever made the postseason in professional baseball, so like a lot of other guys, I went out and celebrated pretty hard that night.

The next day, though, I paid the price with everyone else.

LOSING POSTURE

Tired and a little hungover, we didn't put up much of a fight against the Padres the day after we clinched.

We played sloppy ball, made some errors, and didn't score a single run. Most of our starters sat, but the fans seemed to excuse our performance.

But even though the game didn't have any significance at all toward making the postseason, Lou wasn't at all pleased.

After the game, he came storming into the clubhouse.

"Listen to me right now," he said. "I will not let this team go into the playoffs in a losing posture. I will not."

That's what made Lou such a great manager. He was looking out for us, even when we weren't.

POSTSEASON PINCH

As happy as we were to make it to the playoffs, we were all a bit bummed when the postseason rosters were announced.

Tim Layana had pitched in 55 games in 1990 and was on the roster every day of the season. He was a rookie, but he posted a solid 3.49 ERA and got us out of some jams numerous times. In fact, he was kind of the forgotten member of the Nasty Boys. Norm, Dibs, and Randy considered him one of them.

However, when the playoff roster was posted, Tim's name was left off. In his place, they added some pitchers who could start in a pinch.

You learn a lot about people by the way they handle adversity. And Tim handled it like a guy 15 years wiser.

Obviously, he was initially crushed. We tried to console him at first. We knew it couldn't have been easy for him, but soon, we were joking with him like we would anyone else.

One time during the postseason, we were passing around a ball that was going to be signed by the whole team.

"Sorry, Timmy," I said. "This is only for the roster guys."

We all got a good laugh out of it. Tim was a good sport, and I think he appreciated that we didn't treat him like a charity case. Besides, even though he wasn't on the roster, he was right there on the bench with us for the entire postseason.

Unfortunately, Tim died in a car accident in 1999. But we'll always remember him as a great guy, a solid teammate, and an integral part of our championship team.

PLAYOFF PRESSURE

We had a tall task in the NLCS. We were facing the Pittsburgh Pirates, who won the NL East with 95 wins. Their offense was powered by Barry Bonds, Bobby Bonilla, and my high school buddy Andy Van Slyke, and their starting rotation was led by Doug Drabek, who was a 22-game winner and the National League Cy Young Award winner.

Most people considered us an underdog to the Pirates, and I'm not sure why. As far as I could tell, we were pretty evenly matched. Both of us had big offenses, strong starters, and solid bullpens.

I'm not sure if other players would agree with me, but I really felt that most of the pressure that year would come in the playoffs against the Pirates, not in the World Series.

If you make it to the World Series, you're playing until the end whether you win or lose. But if you don't get out of the playoffs, you don't get the pennant or a shot at a title. You go home completely empty-handed.

That, I thought, would be the worst way to go down.

AFFAIR IN THE GLARE

My first postseason start came in Game 2 of the NLCS. It was, without a doubt, the biggest start of my career up until that point. My major league debut and those Opening Day starts didn't even compare.

The game started at 3 p.m. to accommodate TV coverage. It was the first time we started a game at that time, and it wreaked havoc in the field. The sun poked through the gaps in Riverfront Stadium's upper sections and absolutely blinded us.

The T-shirt says it all: The Pirates couldn't touch Billy Doran, me, or the rest of the Reds in the 1990 NLCS. *Photo courtesy of the Cincinnati Reds*

"If someone lines one up the middle," I told someone between innings, "I'm a dead man. I'll never see it coming."

I dropped my hat low over my forehead so I could see Joe Oliver behind the plate. I struggled just to see the signs.

The other thing that threw me off was the time between innings. Again, because of the TV coverage, we had three minutes between innings. Not only did I work quickly, but I also warmed up quickly. I actually had to wait in the dugout for a couple minutes before I went out to the mound to warm up. It only took me a minute, and I didn't want to stand out there with nothing to do for the other two.

Despite the distractions, I pitched six innings and gave up just one run.

I get doused after we beat the Pirates in the 1990 NLCS. *Photo courtesy of the Cincinnati Reds*

And as it turned out, the sun became a bigger problem for the Pirates than us. In the fifth inning, Paul O'Neill hit a shot that Barry Bonds lost in the sun, which allowed us to score the winning run in our 2-1 victory.

PENNANT WINNERS

We dropped the first game of the NLCS to the Pirates, but rebounded for three straight victories. Ultimately, we clinched the pennant in six games, thanks largely to a dominating performance by the Nasty Boys. The trio allowed just one earned run in 15⅔ innings.

It was great to win the pennant at home in front of our fans. It was a crazy time with a sort of excitement most of us had never experienced. And we were just happy to keep the streak going.

The celebration eventually found its way to Flannigans, a bar not too far from the stadium.

The place was absolutely packed to the rafters with Reds fans. Debbie was pregnant and at home, so I met up with Hal Morris and his mom to celebrate our victory.

For most of the night, we were relegated to the bar's kitchen area. I think they feared a riot if too many fans saw us. We sat back there for most of the night tossing back cold ones. And we, of course, never paid for a single drink.

We poked our heads out every once in a while to see and hear the crowd. It was just an amazing day for the fans.

Any fear or anxiety about the World Series wouldn't be felt until the next morning, when all of those beers finally wore off. For one night, we were just going to savor being National League champions.

GOLIATH COMES TO RIVEFRONT

The Oakland A's entered the 1990 World Series with three consecutive American League pennants.

Their reputation preceded them. They were just an intimidating bunch. Not only had they won 103 games, but they had the AL MVP (Rickey Henderson), the AL Cy Young winner (27-game winner Bob Welch), 22-game winner Dave Stewart, and, of course, the Bash Brothers—Mark McGwire and Jose Canseco.

That slugging duo struck fear in every pitcher's heart.

Prior to Game 1 of the Series, we watched with our jaws on the ground as McGwire and Canseco released an all-out assault on the red seats in Riverfront. Shot after shot pummeled the upper deck, and they seemed to do it with ease. I had never seen one guy—let alone two of them—pound baseballs so effortlessly (of course, based on what we know now, I'm guessing they had some help).

But we knew our brand of baseball was as good as anyone's. We probably had more speed than anyone that year, and we seemed to have the right mix of everything else to compete with any team they could throw at us.

We entered the Series huge underdogs, but we had Goliath in our crosshairs.

SETTING THE STAGE

With one swing of his bat, Eric Davis set the stage for the entire World Series.

Eric was one of our leaders in 1990. Silent, but deadly.

He was also injured. By the World Series, Eric could barely tie his shoes because his left shoulder was aching so badly from a September collision with the outfield wall. He just played the game so hard.

Earlier in the NLCS, Eric had gunned down a runner at third with one of the greatest outfield assists I've seen. But the best was yet to come.

With one on and two out in the first inning of Game 1, Eric blasted a pitch from Dave Stewart deep into center field.

I'll never forget the crowd's reaction. I swear, you could feel Riverfront Stadium shaking. People were screaming and jumping up and down, and it felt like the entire place was swaying under our feet. It was absolutely deafening.

That quickly, it was like we found a chink in Oakland's armor. We were supposed to be huge underdogs, and before people had even finished purchasing their beers and hot dogs, Davis had put us ahead. It's like the entire momentum of the Series swung in our favor.

Behind seven shutout innings by Jose Rijo, we went on to win Game 1 7-0. But it all started with Eric's big home run.

ALL-POINTS BULLETIN

The second game of the World Series was one of the most exciting, and for me, it had nothing to do with what happened on the field. Debbie was eight months pregnant and looked like she could pop at any moment.

With Oakland leading 4-3 in the seventh inning, clubhouse manager Rick Stowe came up to the dugout to find me.

"Hey, Puggy," he said. "Debbie's gone into labor. She needs you."

I ran straight down the tunnel to the clubhouse and didn't even have time to change.

Debbie was at the game, and when she realized she was about to give birth, she took off for the hospital by herself. Unfortunately, her car was blocked in. But Mark Stowe, who was Rick's brother and the assistant clubhouse manager, helped us move the other vehicle out of the way, and Debbie and I were off for the hospital.

After I had filled out the forms and they began preparing Debbie for a Caesarian section, I finally had some time to collect my thoughts. And I soon realized that I hadn't really told anyone I was leaving. But surely, I thought, they'd ask around and find out why I wasn't there.

Soon, the phones at the hospital started ringing nonstop.

"Tom, it's the team," a nurse said. "What do I tell them?"

"They probably just want to know if it's a boy or a girl," I said. "Tell them I'm not here."

I was pacing around the place like a nervous wreck, excited about my new son, worried about Debbie, and stressed about what was happening back at the stadium.

A doctor then came in and said it'd be awhile before Debbie was ready. He then asked if I wanted to watch the rest of the game from the doctors' lounge.

Still in uniform, I walked into the room and flipped on the TV. The Reds had tied it up, and not a minute later, Tim McCarver issued an all-points bulletin.

"Tom, if you're out there and listening, Lou Piniella needs you to come back to the stadium to pitch," he said.

I had no clue what to do. I was scheduled to start Game 3, but if we went into extra innings, they could have decided to use anyone to pitch, including me.

I started to walk to the door, then back to the TV, then to the nurses' station, and then I started looking for the doctor. I was walking in circles. My heart was racing and felt like it was ready to shoot out of my chest.

Then, Joe Oliver came through with the biggest clutch hit of my life, singling to left to score Billy Bates. The game was over, and I was saved.

Two minutes later, the doctor came into the lounge.

"She's ready," he said. "Let's go have a baby."

Soon after, I was a proud father once again. It was just a roller coaster of emotions that ended with the greatest sense of relief a guy could feel.

I spent the night with Debbie and my new son, Tucker, who's still known around town as the "World Series Baby." And then with just one hour of sleep, I headed back to the stadium for our flight to Oakland.

Once there, Lou pulled me aside and congratulated me.

"And damn it, if you ever have to take off like that again, just tell someone!" he said.

I just shook my head in agreement and handed Lou a candy cigar.

ALL-AMERICA PERFORMANCE

One of the greatest performances that kind of became lost in the drama of Game 2 was Jack Armstrong's work out of the bullpen.

For most of the season, Jack "The All-American Boy" (as Marty Brennaman called him) was in the starting rotation, and at the break, he was our best pitcher with an 11-3 record and 2.28 ERA. He even started the All-Star Game that year. But he won just one game in the second half and was moved to the bullpen for the postseason.

In Game 2, our starter, Danny Jackson, got hammered and was pulled after 2⅔ innings. Scott Scudder shut them down for an inning and a third, and then Jack came in to pitch the fifth.

We were only trailing by a run, and Jack kept it close. In his third and final inning that game, he struck out Mark McGwire and Jose Canseco, and he got Willie Randolph to fly out. They were huge outs.

In all, Jack faced just 10 batters in his three innings, and he was arguably the MVP of that game.

But that was typical of our team. Guys always seemed to find a way to contribute, even when most people had written them off.

SCHOTTZIE'S FAREWELL

We had boarded our plane to head for Oakland and Game 3 of the World Series when a big hairy mass came huffing down the aisle.

Once we saw its happy owner holding a leash, we knew right away what it was: Marge's St. Bernard, Schottzie.

I'm sure Schottzie was a great dog, but that damn thing followed us everywhere—batting practice, press conferences, and even team photos. Do you know how hard it is to get 30 or 40 players and coaches to line-up correctly for a photo? Well, imagine throwing an easily distracted 170-pound dog into the mix.

But the fans really loved Schottzie. Hell, I think he had more endorsement deals than anyone on the 25-man roster.

But luckily, Schottzie wasn't heading to Oakland with us. Marge said he just wanted to tell everyone good luck, and she told us all to give him a rub for good luck.

And just to play it safe, she made sure to bring along some baggies full of Schottzie fur for us to use in a pinch.

ONE TO GO

Pitching in Game 3 of the World Series was like walking into a lion's den with loin chops strapped to my body.

To get onto the field at Oakland Coliseum, you had to walk through a center field fence. It felt like I was entering Goliath's living room as I walked onto the field.

We were sitting pretty with a two-game lead in the Series, and it was now up to me to keep the momentum going.

Luckily, our offense provided all the help I needed, thanks to a seven-run third inning. What should have been the most intense and dramatic game of my life had just gotten a whole lot easier. I loved pitching with a lead. I just got aggressive and concentrated on not walking anyone.

"Just throw strikes," I told myself.

Chris Sabo went on to hit two home runs, while Dibs and Randy Myers conserved the lead. We ultimately won 8-3 and took a three-games-to-none lead in the Series.

And we knew history was on our side. Up until that point, no team had ever come back from that type of deficit in a seven-game series.

One more win, and we'd be champions of the world.

SABO'S WORLD

In Game 4, we were trailing 1-0 in the eighth inning before a force play and a sacrifice fly got us a couple runs. We entered the ninth inning clinging to a 2-1 lead, and we were all standing on the top step of the dugout waiting for Randy Myers to get the final three outs.

Well, almost all of us were on the top step.

Chris Sabo was still on the bench, with a bat between his legs while he stared straight at the ground.

"C'mon guys, we can do it!" he said, still looking at the ground. "I know we can! We can win this!"

I looked over at Ronnie.

"Who in the hell is he talking to?" I asked.

"I have no clue," he said.

But that was Sabes. Even when he was just three outs away from a World Series title, he was still in a world all his own.

WORLD SERIES MVP

Oakland ran into an absolute buzz saw in Jose Rijo, who got the Game 4 win after Randy Myers closed it out.

And thanks to his other win in Game 1, Rijo was named the World Series MVP.

It was a remarkable turnaround, especially when you consider that he was nearly yanked from the starting rotation just a couple months prior.

One day in August, our pitching coach called all of the starters into the outfield during batting practice for a quick meeting.

"I talked to Lou, and we're thinking of shifting to a four-man rotation down the stretch," Stan Williams told us.

Everyone was fine with the decision, and Jose said he agreed.

"I'm glad to hear that, Jose," Steamer said. "Because you're the one we're going to bump from the rotation."

I think Jose was a little blindsided. He hadn't been pitching poorly, but no one could seem to light a fire under his butt. He was a pretty easygoing guy, but I think Lou and the coaches thought he was a little too easygoing.

Obviously, their plan worked, and it seemed to really spark something in Jose. He stayed in the rotation, going 6-2 in his final eight regular-season starts, which was followed by one of the most dominant World Series performances I've ever seen.

A DAY OF CELEBRATION

After the final out of the World Series, we headed back to the clubhouse for a celebration that would last for the next 24 hours.

The champagne was poured immediately. Everyone was celebrating. I had never seen anything like it. Even Rickey Henderson and some of the A's came into the clubhouse to congratulate us. It was just a rowdy and wild time.

Eventually, we headed to the hotel bar to continue the celebration. As soon as we got there, I heard Steve Schott tell the bartender to pay for one round and then close out the tab. So basically, we were left to pay for our own World Series party.

Steve was Marge's nephew. He wasn't a bad guy, but he just had no baseball sense, so I never understood why he went to work for the team. I remember him asking Joe Nuxhall one time what he did before he was a broadcaster.

It didn't matter, though. No one could ruin our good time.

Afterward, a few guys headed to their rooms to catch some sleep before our flight, but the majority of us just continued drinking and celebrating.

We soon made our way to the airport for the flight home. I had never sensed so much excitement and energy before on one of our flights. We had finally gotten over the state of shock and were deep into celebration mode.

I remember sitting in the airplane's galley (a sort of service elevator for food, drinks, and other supplies) with Rick Stowe and Reds minority owner George Strike. Don't ask how we ended up there—I have no idea. We were just swept up the moment. I think we were all on the verge of tears, double-fisting bottles of champagne.

During the whole time, I never did get any sleep. So by the time I made it back home, I was ready for a long and needed night of rest. But I couldn't have possibly gone to bed any happier.

WHITE HOUSE, RED CHEEK

After we won the Series, we received the customary invitation to the White House so we could meet the president, who back in 1990, was George H.W. Bush.

I had planned to leave Washington D.C. as soon as we were finished, so I could do some elk hunting in Wyoming.

We were headed to the White House when Marge walked to the back of the bus to talk to me.

I had grown a beard to help keep me warm for my hunting trip, and Marge gave it a small tug.

"What's this, honey?" she asked.

The Reds had a long-standing ban on facial hair, but the season was obviously over.

"That's a beard, Marge," I said.

"Remember, you're on *my* time now, Toots."

And with that comment, she reared up and slapped me right across the face.

I wasn't surprised, though. If there was anything I had learned during my six seasons in Cincinnati, it was how to press Marge's buttons. And it occasionally earned me a red cheek.

PRIME TIME

Our team in 1990 was literally in the prime of our lives.

I've always considered the ages of 26 to 30 to be the most promising time in a player's baseball career. And if you look at our roster from 1990, you'll see that nine out of 10 guys fell into the magic range.

In fact, our entire starting eight was under the age of 30, and other than Rick Mahler, I was the old man in the rotation at the rather youthful age of 30.

Guys like Ronnie Oester, Eric Davis, Paul O'Neill, and me—guys who would have been youngsters on any other team—found ourselves in veteran leadership roles in 1990.

You saw guys like Eric and Paul take that experience and excel in other cities, and I think Ronnie and I did a pretty good job holding down the fort back here at home in the years that followed.

But it all started in 1990 with what's surely Cincinnati's youngest championship team.

1990 VERSUS THE MACHINE

The city of Cincinnati loves its World Series winners.

But once we won the title, the comparisons started almost immediately. Fans and the media started discussing right away how we compared to the city's previous World Series winners—the 1976 Big Red Machine.

Despite our success, the general consensus was that there was no comparison. Most people thought we weren't even in the same class.

That's always kind of bugged me.

Granted, the Reds team that won the Series in 1976 (and 1975) had what is, perhaps, the greatest starting eight ever assembled. They had three Hall of Famers (Joe Morgan, Johnny Bench, and Tony Perez) and two that should be (Pete Rose and Davey Concepcion). And the rest of the guys (Ken Griffey, George Foster, and Cesar Geronimo) were perennial All-Stars and not exactly scrap-heap material.

I still say that our team had better pitching, though. And our offense in 1990 could compete with anyone past or present. Other teams may have scored more runs, but we seemed to score them when they mattered most. We didn't have any potential Hall of Famers (other than Barry

Larkin), but just about everyone peaked during that season. And I can't think of a team deeper or more balanced than our squad.

But it's a stupid argument to try to make either way. If nothing else, the teams of 1976 and 1990 prove there's more than one way to go about winning a title.

TOO MANY MEMORIES

When you look at the stats from the 1990 season, no single person really sticks out. No one on our team hit 30 home runs, knocked in more than 100 runs, or even scored 100 runs.

We didn't have a single pitcher with more than 15 wins, and not one of us won a major award or led the league in a major statistical category.

But give me the name of anyone on our roster, and I'll tell you something big he did during the season. Everyone played a vital role in our success that year. Never have I seen so many different people contribute in so many different ways.

That's the type of environment that creates true team camaraderie. No one slacked off or didn't do his share. We knew that each guy in the dugout had done something to get us a World Series title. That's why I'll always consider the 1990 Cincinnati Reds my favorite team that I've ever been a part of.

I tried to mention as many of my teammates as I could in this chapter, because frankly, every guy from our championship team deserves some recognition. I could devote an entire book simply to our unforgettable season. Unfortunately, I was limited to just one chapter, and all the great memories I accumulated during the 1990 season could never fit into such a small space.

10

WORLD SERIES HANGOVER

FAILED NEGOTIATION

Soon after we celebrated winning the 1990 World Series, reality sunk in: I didn't have a contract for 1991.

Especially by this time, I was determined to finish my career in a Cincinnati uniform. But I think the Reds knew that, and I had to be careful that they didn't take advantage of my loyalty.

One night Marge took my wife and me out to dinner at the Cincinnatian to see if we could figure out something. We weren't on the same page, though. The Giants were offering me a pretty big deal at the time, and the Reds weren't even close to matching it.

We left dinner knowing that my career in Cincinnati was probably over. Marge knew it, too. By the time we got to the coat check, she was fuming. So she slapped me. This time, it didn't seem like a playful slap, though. I think she really meant business.

"Talk some sense into him!" she said, looking to my wife.

Debbie never wanted to leave. We had built a home just across the river in Kentucky. My kids were in school, and their friends were here. It had really become our home. But Debbie understood the business.

"I'm sorry, Marge. I go where he goes," she said.

Marge knew she had most of the wives in her back pocket. It was her trump card. But this time, it did her no good, and I don't think a single person left our dinner happy.

I had more riding on the line than my own interests, though. I wasn't looking out just for my family and me, but also for every player in my category. One contract can completely change the landscape of free agency, and if I took less than the going rate, I knew it could affect guys throughout all of professional baseball. I just couldn't take that risk.

BACK WITH CINCINNATI

It was Thanksgiving, and I had finally accepted the fact that I'd be leaving the Reds and taking San Francisco's five-year deal. It was a sad time for the entire family. Our run with the Reds was over.

My agent, Jim Bronner, flew into town, and I was getting ready to head over to the Westin to pick him up. We were going to come back to the house so we could call the Giants and accept their offer.

As I threw on some clothes, Debbie was in the kitchen preparing Thanksgiving dinner and started to cry. We just couldn't believe it was actually happening. I left the house before the emotions got to me, too.

I made it to the hotel, and I was at Jim's door and ready to knock when I heard him yelling.

"Bob, you know what Tom means to this team!" he screamed.

It was obvious he was on the phone talking to Reds general manager Bob Quinn.

I wasn't sure what to do, so I just went to the lobby and waited for him. It was an emotional time. I guess I just never thought my time in Cincinnati would come to an end.

A little while later, Jim showed up, and he didn't look at all pleased. I assumed he gave the Reds a final shot at making a new offer, but it was apparent it didn't work.

We got into my truck and were headed back to my house.

"We need to stop by the stadium first," Jim said.

I was a little embarrassed. I hadn't gotten a haircut or shaved in nearly two months, and I was wearing a pair of torn jeans and an old T-shirt. Had Jim really gotten Marge to change her mind?

We walked into her office, and Marge told me she reconsidered and was offering a four-year deal with an option for a fifth. The money was nearly identical to the Giants' offer.

I was thrilled. We were staying in Cincinnati, and most likely, it would be for the remainder of my career.

Marge could have held a grudge for having to budge on her offer, and I probably wouldn't have blamed her. She was close to my family, but I wouldn't have been at all surprised if the whole episode caused a rift in our friendship. Baseball can be a tough business. But instead, Marge let me know there were no hard feelings.

"I'm glad we could work it out, honey," she said, giving me a hug.

DEFENDING CHAMPS

With my new contract, I entered spring training a pretty happy camper. Not only had we taken care of the contract, but we were also the defending champs. Almost everyone was coming back for the 1991 season, and I was sure we could make a run at a second title.

Sure, there was some pressure. No defending champions can enter the season without having high expectations placed upon them. We were no different. After beating the Pirates for the National League pennant, we swept the A's even though we were huge underdogs. I think people really started to appreciate and respect the talent we had on the team.

Unfortunately, any hopes of a repeat title disappeared midway through the season. We became absolutely decimated by injuries. Most of our regulars were on the shelf, and we were soon using a roster full of Class AAA guys.

It was a disappointing way to follow up our championship season. But if nothing else, the season was good for some great stories and plenty of laughs.

FOOL ME ONCE...

One of our best pranks (and probably second-best) targeted Glenn Sutko, a young catcher who enjoyed two short stints with the Reds in 1990 and 1991.

We convinced him that Glenn Braggs, our resident muscle man, was so strong that he could lift three guys high enough off the ground that someone could roll a baseball under them.

Sutko seemed skeptical, but everyone in the clubhouse was in on the prank. And we were quite convincing.

"I'll bet $100 Braggsy can't do it!" someone yelled.

"I have a $100 that says he can!" someone else said.

By then, everyone was yelling out predictions. Sutko's face lit up at the possibility that maybe Braggs was actually strong enough to do it.

We grabbed a bar and looked for three volunteers. We told Sutko to take the middle spot since he was a big guy and probably weighed a lot. Two guys then got on both sides of him, and they locked arms and legs with him. Sutko didn't realize it, but he was trapped with no way to get free.

While Braggs acted like he was stretching and getting ready for the lift, other guys ran off to grab bottles of whatever they could find.

We yelled, "One! Two!"

And right before we got to three, someone unbuckled Sutko's pants, and we rained down a parade of ketchup, mustard, baby powder, shampoo—anything and everything we could find in the clubhouse.

The poor guy was caked in a couple inches of the most unbelievably foul mixture of crap you'd ever seen.

He just laughed and hung his head in embarrassment, knowing he had made a rookie mistake.

FOOL ME TWICE

In camp the next year, Sutko came up to me and said he wanted to get another rookie with our power-lifting prank.

"Great!" I said. "You'll be one of the guys on the end of that bar since you know how it works."

We even let him pick out a target. I can't even remember who it was now. But we immediately let the new guy know what was going on.

We went through the same spiel as before, and everyone huddled around.

Sutko smirked, no doubt excited about his part in the rookie hazing. "One! Two!"

And before he knew what hit him, Sutko was again showered with the same condiments and toiletries. We erupted into laughter, and Sutko just sat there wondering how he could have fallen for the same prank twice.

Some guys just never learn.

ALL-STAR CONTROVERSY

My only All-Star appearance came in 1991, but it didn't come without controversy.

We were in second place, eight games above .500 through the first half of the season, and we had plenty of guys who deserved a spot on the All-Star team. And because the Reds had won the World Series the year before, Lou Piniella was skipper of the National League squad. He got to pick the pitchers and the reserve position players for his team.

Chris Sabo was voted in by the fans, so he was a lock. Lou then selected Barry Larkin, Paul O'Neill, Rob Dibble, and me to fill out the NL roster.

It's a tough job, deciding the players you think are worthy. Obviously some deserving guys are going to be left off of the rosters every year. There are only so many spots to go around.

But I felt that all of Lou's picks were warranted. I had a record of 10-4 with a 3.76 ERA when he added me the team, so I had no doubt in my mind that I deserved a spot. And I can say the same about Lark, Paul, and Dibs.

And besides, league president Bill White had to sign off on all of the picks, and he specifically stated that Lou had no reason to apologize for any of his choices.

But Braves manager Bobby Cox didn't agree. He was upset that Terry Pendleton was left off of the roster. Pendleton was hitting .324 at the time, but Howard Johnson beat him out for the reserve spot at third base. Bobby thought that Lou had picked too many Reds players, which ate up a spot that could have been used for Terry. I can't blame Bobby for being upset, though. In fact, I think any good manager is expected to stand up for his players like that. I'm sure Terry appreciated it.

However, I guess you could say that a benefit of winning the World Series is that you can reward your own guys. And it's not like Lou was the first guy to do that. Every skipper who manages the All-Star team takes a lot of his own guys. It's been like that for years. Hell, even Bobby's done it.

Regardless of the grumblings around the league, I was just happy to finally make the team. I think it's a goal of any major leaguer to make at least one All-Star team, and I was going to enjoy it no matter what anyone thought.

MEETING MR. GUNK BALL

It's hard to imagine anything more exciting than being in an All-Star clubhouse. You're surrounded by the best baseball has to offer, and you actually get the humbling experience of being one of them—for a day, anyway.

The All-Star Game was held in Toronto in 1991, and I was really looking forward to it. You hear about how great the whole All-Star experience is from other guys, but you always want to experience it for yourself.

One of the first guys I saw when I walked into the NL clubhouse was Dennis Martinez, a well-known curveball specialist from the Montreal Expos.

Dennis used to chew a mouthful of tobacco, and a lot of people thought that he used to get a wad of that sticky gunk on the ball, which I'm sure gave his curve a little more bite.

He never got called out on it, so I used to tease him about it all the time. Once I saw him in the clubhouse, I didn't utter a word. I just did my best impersonation of him, acting like I was chewing a big wad of tobacco and spitting fake loogies on a ball.

He got a kick out of it. Everyone kidded around in the clubhouse like that.

That was one of the great things about the All-Star Game. When else would I get the opportunity to joke around with guys who are supposed to be my opponents? All year, I'm supposed to be battling against the guys. But even All-Stars are fans of the game.

But for one game, I actually got to call them teammates and have some fun.

BORN-AGAIN ROOKIE

The All-Star Game was held on a Tuesday at the Skydome. I had made a start two days earlier for the Reds, so I knew I wasn't really slated to pitch in the game. I was the extra-innings guy, the one they saved in case the All-Star Game went longer than nine innings. (Too bad I wasn't around when they ran out of pitchers in the 2002 All-Star Game.)

So, I was really able to just kind of relax and soak in the whole experience.

We were treated like royalty that week. They gave us all kinds of gifts. We even got paintings of ourselves to commemorate our All-Star years.

I was really excited to meet guys like Eddie Murray, Ryne Sanberg, and Ozzie Smith, perennial All-Stars I used to look up to when I was still trying to make it to the pros.

I was just 31 that season, but I still felt like a rookie around those guys. I guess every guy probably feels that way during his first All-Star Game.

One of the greatest guys I met during the festivities was Lee Smith. Lee was a dominating closer during the 1980s and 1990s, and it was great to hang out and talk to him about how he goes about his job.

Lee and I spent the last few innings together in the bullpen. I told him about one of the scariest at-bats I ever had. It was against him. He was pitching for the Cubs, and this was before they had installed lights at Wrigley Field. By the time he came into the game, it was pretty late, and there wasn't much natural light. And I'm trying to find a 100-mile-per-hour fastball coming from Lee, a guy six and a half feet tall. I was scared to death. He thought it was hilarious when I told him about it.

We ended up losing the All-Star Game 4-2, but I couldn't have asked for a better couple of days. I met some great people, enjoyed a few days as a superstar, and I earned the right to always call myself an All-Star. That's the great thing about it. No matter if you were on 20 All-Star teams or just one, you're always called an All-Star.

TALE OF TWO SEASONS

Except for that demotion to the minors in 1987, I was enjoying a nice and productive run as a Reds starter. I won at least 15 games from 1988 to 1990, and I was well on pace again in 1991.

But right before the All-Star break, I injured my hip. I didn't tell anyone, though—even as the pain continued throughout the second half of the season.

I never mentioned the injury because I was pretty embarrassed about how it happened. I broke my own rule of not going out on nights I didn't pitch, and I paid the price.

We were down in Houston, and after a game, a few of us headed to a local watering hole. On the way out, a few guys recognized us as ballplayers, and they started jawing with us. I told everyone to keep walking, but one of my dumber teammates confronted the loudest one.

Before I knew it, a brawl had broken out, and I got pushed from behind. I remember looking down to see my brand new Rolex, a gift from my wife after I signed my contract, all busted up.

As we tried to break things up and leave, my leg got caught under me, and I felt a sharp twinge in my hip. I wasn't scheduled to pitch for another two days, so I just hoped the pain would be gone by then.

But it wasn't. And it didn't really get any better during the rest of the season. I pitched with pain down the stretch and kept it to myself.

Prior to the All-Star break, I was 10-4, and I remember reading a newspaper story recapping our first half. It said another 15-win season by me was a lock. Sadly, I never reached the mark.

I was on pace for perhaps my best season since I went 20-9 as a rookie, but as fate would have it, I finished the second half with a 4-10 record and an overall mark of 14-14. It was the first season I didn't have a winning record since 1987.

I was really disappointed with the whole year. Our 1991 season was just a debacle, and I was hoping I could provide some relief while everyone else was injured. As it turned out, I got injured myself, but kept pitching. I had never been on the disabled list, and I guess I was just too proud to consider going on it.

PERFECT TOMMY'S

One night, Scott Scudder, Rick Stowe, and I went to a bar called Blondies in New York. We chatted up the bartender, and I learned that he went to Tennessee Wesleyan, the same school I went to for my senior year of college. That wasn't the only thing that hit close to home, though.

While there, we met some people who told us about a bar where all of the soap-opera stars hung out. As baseball players, we had most of our early afternoons free, so we were soap-opera connoisseurs of sorts.

"Well, you guys should come check it out with us," a girl said. "It's called Perfect Tommy's."

"Perfect Tommy's?" I asked, almost hysterical. "Are you serious?"

I was just three years removed from my perfect game, so I of course wanted to see the place for myself.

Sure enough, we went to the bar, and it was just swarming with our daytime favorites. We were then introduced to the owner of the bar, who was wearing a leather jacket with a big "Perfect Tommy's" insignia on it. It was the coolest jacket I had ever seen, and I really wanted it.

"I'll give you $3,000 for it right now," I said.

And I was serious. I was young and dumb, and after signing my big contract earlier that year, I sometimes spent lavishly on stupid items. But this one wasn't completely stupid. I was proud of my perfect game, and I knew I'd get one hell of a reaction if I could wear the jacket into the clubhouse.

Unfortunately, the guy turned down my offer. He wouldn't budge. He told me about some catalog where you could order one, but like any impulse buy, I forgot about it soon after.

BRUISED AND BEATEN

The injury bug was just merciless in 1991. Eric Davis, Barry Larkin, Chris Sabo, Jose Rijo, Norm Charlton, Scott Scudder, Chris Hammond—all of them were hit by it at some point. And there were many more.

With so many guys shelved at some point during the season, we soon fell out of the pennant race and dropped way under .500 in the second half. It was so discouraging.

The toughest thing about losing is that it becomes contagious. When you're injured, beaten, and just down on your luck, you come to the ballpark expecting to lose. You expect the worst. "How are we going to blow it today?" you think.

And it rubs off. Soon, those doubts and frustrations hit everyone in the clubhouse. No one believes the team can win, and you just seem to wait for the next injury to pop up.

Baseball's a humbling game. Just when you think you have it figured out, the baseball gods hear you and show you that you really don't.

It was especially tough in 1991, just one year after we won the World Series.

By the All-Star break, we climbed well over .500, but once the injuries hit, we tanked and plummeted in the standings. Everyone was getting injured, and soon we were fielding a Class AAA team.

Any season like that is tough, but when it comes just one year after you win the World Series, it just makes it even tougher to swallow.

NEVER SAW THE WALL

The players weren't the only ones getting banged up that year.

As I've said before, College Nights at the ballpark were always pretty rowdy.

One time the vast outfield seating section of the stadium was empty, but a kid found his way up to vacant sections and started hauling butt across the upper deck.

It was obvious he had been drinking, considering the zigzag route he was taking across the outfield sections.

Back then it wasn't really considered a security threat like it is nowadays when stuff like that happens. We didn't really worry when we saw something strange like that; we'd just wait for security to round them up, and then we'd go back to business as usual. But things didn't end so quietly this night.

Once everyone realized what was going on, a cop took off after the guy.

That's when the crowd came to life, and it sounded like the last leg of the Kentucky Derby. As the cop got closer and closer, the roar from the fans got louder and louder.

The cop was gaining ground, and the drunk fan looked back to see how big of a lead he had. He kept watching the cop, almost like he was taunting him. You could tell he was getting a kick out of the whole thing.

Unfortunately, the guy never paid attention to what was in front of him.

By the time he turned back around, he had run face first into a wall at full steam. It nearly knocked him out. He looked lifeless.

The crowd was just merciless that night, laughing and cheering. Even the guys in the dugout had to laugh. There's just something about watching drunk people hurt themselves that makes you crack up.

Luckily, they had padded the walls in Riverfront Stadium by then, so the guy seemed okay after a while, and they hauled him off to the drunk tank. But I'm sure the guy was feeling a little sore in the morning.

PROFESSOR LOU

As trying an experience as the 1991 season was for the guys in the dugout, it had to have been doubly tough for Lou. He went from leading a team to the World Series to trying to keep us out of last place.

Lou, obviously, had a lot to complain about in 1991. If we weren't injured, we were finding ways to blow leads and lose games we should have won. Everything that went right in 1990 seemed to go wrong in 1991.

It got to Lou, and he yelled a lot that year. Occasionally, he'd call some guys out. But Lou never did it maliciously or to embarrass anyone. If he called you out, he'd make sure everyone heard. He wanted it to become a lesson for everyone. We all learned from each other's mistakes.

Lou just didn't stand idle when mediocrity was setting in or when he saw a lack of effort. He demanded 100 percent at all times. He knew it was the only way we'd play our best.

In 1990, I thought Lou was a great manager. He led us to the World Series, and he got the most out of us. But it was only after I saw Lou during those troubling times of 1991 that I learned he was the complete package. Even during the tough times, he kept the lessons coming and never settled for anything but our best effort.

That's why I always say Lou was the best manager I ever had. He might not have been the guy I was closest with or my favorite manager (that was Pete), but he was undoubtedly my best manager. And I'm sure just about any guy who's played for him will say the same.

STRANGE BREW

When reliever Steve Foster made his debut with the Reds in 1991, it almost became an international incident.

The Reds farm hand learned that he would be getting a September call-up to the majors and would be joining the club during a series in Montreal.

Once he got to Canada, customs officials asked the rookie if he had anything to declare. He told us he had no idea what they meant. He had never traveled internationally, so he wasn't sure what they were asking. So he said the first thing that came to mind.

"Uh, I'm proud to be an American," he boldly declared.

He swears he wasn't trying to be smart with the officials, but they just didn't find the humor in his response and detained him for a little longer than usual.

But when he finally made it to the clubhouse and explained what happened, we knew he'd fit in just fine.

CAGE RAGE

Another of the Class AAA guys who got a shot after all those injuries in 1991 was Gino Minutelli, a left-handed pitcher I hadn't seen since camp. But how could I forget Gino?

Back in spring training, the pitchers threw batting practice to the hitters. Unfortunately for Gino, he had some weird phobia or something that made it impossible for him to throw into the batting cage. I mean it's a batting cage. It's probably 30 feet wide and 20 feet tall, but he couldn't throw a ball in it to save his life. It was one of the strangest things I had ever seen. The ball would go left and right and over the cage, but never in it. The harder he tried, the more frustrated he got. It was like something straight out of *Major League*.

However, once we started playing regular spring games (and put away the cages), Gino pitched just fine. He even nearly made the team out of camp.

But I never did figure out why he couldn't throw in the cage.

THRIFTY THREADS

With so many new guys joining the club in 1991, our rookie hazing nearly became a full-time job.

It's a rite of passage for rookies to have to endure a little humiliation. It was nothing too bad—just something to cause a little embarrassment. It was all in good fun, and nobody ever got too bent out of shape about it.

One of our favorite traditions was shopping for new outfits for the rookies. We'd go to the same thrift shop in Atlanta whenever we were in town and buy the most awful-looking threads we could find.

Once the rookies were out in the field, we'd clean out their lockers and leave just the clothes we bought. So when we took off for the next city on our road trip, the guys were forced to wear the new threads or go naked. It was always fun to watch the reactions from people out in public.

You couldn't even imagine how terrible some of those outfits were. They looked like they came straight out of Kent Tekulve's closet. The stuff was made of fabrics and materials that probably don't even exist anymore.

But as bad as those guys had it, I suppose it could have been worse. According to Rick Stowe, who's still the clubhouse manager with the Reds, the 2005 Reds rookies had to travel to one city wearing Hooters waitress outfits.

I'm just mad I didn't think of doing that to our guys.

WILD TURKEY

We were hosting the Expos one time, and it just kept raining and raining. We were down a run, and then we had a two-hour rain delay. We played another inning, and then we had another rain delay. The whole thing dragged on and on.

It was just a miserable night, and Lou seemed pretty aggravated.

We went back out there to play again, but they finally called it, and the game was over. We lost by a run.

It was after midnight, and everyone was just tired and hungry. So when we saw an amazing spread of turkey, mashed potatoes, and all the fixings waiting for us, we couldn't wait to dig in.

But Lou was still steaming.

"I can't believe anyone feels like eating after that crap tonight!" he yelled.

He took a look at the food, and then he gave the table a swift kick. The whole thing flew over, and the turkey shot into the wall and absolutely exploded. It was like a bomb went off in it.

"Now get the hell out of here!" he screamed.

Lou then stormed out of the lounge.

We all kind of just stood there dumbfounded. As mad as Lou was, seeing that turkey blow up made me want to laugh out loud.

But Randy Myers and Carmelo Martinez were starving, and there was no way they were going to let the turkey go to waste. They grabbed some forks and started eating it off the floor. That lasted for a few minutes until Lou caught them and chased them away.

If nothing else, Lou was an entertaining guy. When a guy wears his heart on his sleeve like he does, there's bound to be some casualties. Luckily for us, it was only a turkey that night.

MY FIRST LONG BALL

I remember Marty Brennaman always saying that I took more pride in my hitting than any pitcher he watched. It was quite the compliment because Marty was right; I did take a lot of pride in it. After all, as a starting pitcher, I only got to play every five days, so I wanted to make the most of my time in the lineup.

All starting pitchers dream about coming through with the big hit in a game. We all want to be home-run hitters. However, it was 1991, I was in my eighth big league season, and I hadn't hit a single home run.

In one of our final games of the season, we were playing the Padres. I walked Tim Teufel with two outs in the inning. He then stole second and later scored when Benito Santiago singled him in.

After the inning, Lou chewed me out for not paying attention to Teufel at first base. He really aired me out. He thought I got careless and didn't keep Teufel close enough to the bag, which allowed him to steal second and end up scoring.

I went to the plate the next inning, and I was mad as hell. I was ticked at giving up the run, and I was ticked I had to hear about it from Lou. So when Jose Melendez offered up a juicy 2-0 fastball, I swung as hard as I could.

I hit the ball perfectly, and it soared toward right field. Once I saw Tony Gwynn stop to watch it, I knew it was gone. It was such a great feeling running around the bases. I didn't trot or flip my bat or anything like that. I didn't want it to look like I was trying to show anyone up. But on the inside, I was doing cartwheels.

I got the ball back after the inning, and I still proudly display it at home. So yes, I was able to protect my first home-run ball better than that perfect-game ball that my kids lost in the backyard. I guess it just goes to show you how much pitchers cherish their long balls.

JOSE CLAUS

At the end of the 1991 season, Jose Rijo dragged around a huge cardboard box looking for donations to take back home with him.

Jose grew up in the Dominican Republic, and he said that even though the country was crazy about baseball, most kids were far too poor to afford the proper equipment. As a teenager trying out for the Yankees, he was using a pair of borrowed cleats that were too small and crushed his feet. Still, though, there were slim pickings, so he was just happy to have any cleats at all.

Even though Jose went on to become a millionaire and one of baseball's best pitchers, he never forgot his roots. At the end of the season, he would scrounge up all of the used equipment he could find to take back with him to the Dominican. I'm sure the kids probably thought he was Santa Claus. We'd make sure that box was stuffed full of our equipment. I remember Eric Davis one year donating two or three dozen pairs of cleats and over 100 batting gloves for the kids in Jose's old neighborhood.

I know a lot of guys thought Jose was kind of loud and overly confident—kinda "flashy." But that was just his persona when he was in uniform.

In real life, he was a true national treasure.

HOOP DREAMS

I love basketball. I've always said that if I were just a foot taller, I would have been an NBA All-Star.

Even after I got to the majors, I loved to play, and luckily, so did a lot of my teammates. And because so many of the guys hung around Cincinnati during the offseason, we had a Reds basketball team. We'd play 10 or 15 games during the winter, mostly to raise money for local charities. We drew some pretty big crowds all around the area.

One time we got to play Rick Pitino, the head basketball coach at the University of Kentucky, and his staff down in Lexington.

There was a lot riding on the line. Our guys wanted to be known for something other than just baseball, and Pitino and his guys didn't want to be shown up at their own game by a bunch of ballplayers. They used to play every day at 6 a.m., and I'm sure they thought they'd roll right over us.

But you talk about intensity! At times, it was just a ruthless game. I had the job of guarding Pitino, and our guys—Hal Morris, Eric Davis, Paul O'Neill, and a few others—really went at the rest of them. It was a charity game, but you would have never known by watching it.

We ended up beating them, which was probably the most satisfying victory for our Reds hoops team. It didn't come without some casualties, though. Tim Birtsas rolled his ankle, and I felt so guilty about getting him to play that I kept him at my house for four days to nurse him back to health. If he entered spring training dinged up, I knew they'd point the finger at me.

Not long after that victory, they put the ax on our basketball team. Our contracts were getting too big, and they thought there was too much risk of someone getting seriously hurt.

So Pitino never got a rematch, and we remain 1-0 against the Wildcats.

11

ON THE MEND

BROKEN, NOT BEATEN

On Opening Day in 1992, Joe Nuxhall was given the honor of throwing out the ceremonial first pitch.

That February, Joe had undergone surgery for prostate cancer. For the first time since the 1940s, he arrived late to spring training. But the cancer was diagnosed early, and Joe was as upbeat as ever when he finally made it to camp. We all knew he'd beat it. Joe was a battler like that.

Because I lived in the Cincinnati area during the offseason, I saw just how much support came flooding in when the announcement was made about Joe's cancer. If there were any questions about his popularity with Reds fans, it was soon put to rest. Joe was a true Cincinnati icon.

I was amazed by the way Joe handled it all. I'm sure he was scared and exhausted, but he never gave you the impression anything had changed. He was the same great guy he had always been.

Although I wouldn't suffer anything as serious as cancer, I battled my own troubles from 1992 to 1995. My patience, endurance, and will were all challenged. I had never been on the disabled list once in my entire career up until 1992, but I couldn't seem to stay off of it in the years that followed.

But no matter how discouraged I got, I just thought about the courage that people like Joe demonstrated during their troubling times. I learned a lot about handling my own adversity by remembering how Joe did it.

And whenever I thought I couldn't overcome my problems, I just thought of Joe throwing out that first pitch.

MARTY'S THE MAN

I took pride in the fact that I had never been on the disabled list prior to 1992, even though I probably should have been a few times.

One time in 1991 I had rolled my ankle, and it bothered me for weeks afterward. During my next start, someone chopped a shot just over my head, but because I had little strength in my ankle, I couldn't really jump to make much of an attempt at getting it. After the game, someone mentioned that Marty Brennaman, the Reds' radio play-by-play guy, said it looked like I had made a lazy effort.

Now, I've been blamed for a lot of things in my life, but a lack of effort was never one of them. I took his criticism to heart, and I confronted Marty about it.

Back then, just like today, Marty pretty much said what he thought. Although he's technically an employee of the Reds (and not the radio station) and essentially our coworker, Marty had no problem criticizing a player if he thought it was warranted.

"C'mon, Marty," I said. "My ankle's killing me. I *can't* jump. I know it probably looked like I loafed it, but that's all I had."

Marty never interrupted me or took exception to the confrontation. He listened patiently and intently. He really wanted to hear what I had to say.

When I was finished pleading my case, Marty said he understood and that he never would have made the comment had he known the whole story.

That's what I liked about Marty and why I always had respect for him. While other broadcasters are quick to criticize—and then quick to hide and duck you, Marty always made himself available to anyone who had a bone to pick with him.

As I became a veteran in the Reds clubhouse, I felt comfortable talking to Marty if I thought he was being too tough on one of the younger guys. He didn't always agree with me, and he only backed down if he thought he was wrong, but at least he would hear me out.

All of the good ones were like that. As much as talk-show hosts like Bob Trumpy and Andy Furman can get under players' skins, they'd always face the music. You could always expect them in the clubhouse the following day if you wanted to say something in your defense.

That's what separates the good ones from the bad ones. And that's why Marty and I always had a good relationship. It was built on a mutual respect and understanding.

BIRTHDAY SURPRISE

It was April 28, 1992, and I was celebrating my 32nd birthday by pitching against the Pittsburgh Pirates in Riverfront.

The strike zone was shrinking, and I thought I was getting squeezed. I gave up a run in the fifth and one in the sixth, and when I headed back to the bench afterward, I looked over at Tom Hallion, the home-plate umpire.

"Hey, you know some of those pitches are close," I said.

"What?" Hallion asked, walking toward me.

"Those pitches," I muttered, walking toward the dugout, "some of them are close. Feel free to call them strikes."

And like that, I got tossed from the game. I was irate.

"What?!?!" I screamed. "You couldn't even hear me!"

I was just furious. I went into the dugout and threw a bag of sunflower seeds on the field, and when that didn't make much of an impact, I threw an entire box, nearly taking off the head of Larry Rothschild, our pitching coach. I was stomping around, yelling, screaming—generally making an ass out of myself.

And then it hit me what day it was.

"And you can't toss me," I yelled. "It's my birthday!"

I said it like it would really make Hallion have a change of heart, like it was a legitimate excuse to keep me in there. Hallion didn't seem to care, though. I was sent to the clubhouse, and my day was done.

But the boys came through big time. We were down 2-1, but they scored two runs after I got tossed, and I actually got the win.

How's that for a birthday present?

GATOR BAIT

After 162 regular-season games and nonstop travel for six months, I always looked forward to the offseason and spending time with my family. However, once camp rolled around, I couldn't wait to get back into the clubhouse with all of the guys. Spring training was always a little rowdier because the guys felt like we had to make up for lost time.

One year down in Plant City, Cincinnati's former spring-training home, the guys noticed Marge Schott near the lake between our major league complex and the minor league fields. Marge was a huge animal lover, so she didn't think twice about heading down to the lake when word spread that a local alligator was near the shore.

Once we heard about it in the clubhouse, we had to see for ourselves. Damned if Marge wasn't nearly nose to nose with that gator!

She tried to strike up a conversation—whistling, clapping, anything to get its attention. Luckily (for Marge), it didn't look like the gator was in a big hurry to do much of anything.

That didn't stop me and the guys, though. While Marge flipped pebbles, we chucked boulders. When she whistled, we screamed.

Marge never even noticed. And neither did the gator.

Soon, they both lost interest, and Marge headed back to the clubhouse with all limbs attached.

CAUGHT RED-FACED

By 1992 I had taken up golf, and I was getting pretty good. I only had to pitch every five days, so I could afford some distractions during my downtime. Unfortunately, some of the starters and bench guys were taking up golf, too, and Lou Piniella thought it was causing everyone to lose concentration. So he nixed any golf excursions during our road trips.

Back then Joe Nuxhall and I had become pretty good golf buddies. The golf ban obviously didn't apply to Joe, but he wasn't too thrilled to lose the majority of guys he played with.

However, Joe and I had a few tricks up our sleeves. We'd have Bernie Stowe, the clubhouse manager, ship our golf clubs to our destination city separate from the regular equipment. We'd sneak out and play, and Lou would be none the wiser.

The plan worked for a while—until one fateful day in San Francisco.

Joe and I went down to Stanford Golf Course, where the sun was just brutal. It was only an hour or so from San Francisco, but it was a lot sunnier down there. Neither of us wore a hat, so when Joe first got to the clubhouse later that afternoon, he was already burnt to a crisp.

Lou saw him, and he must have thought it was odd, seeing how San Francisco was cloudy that day.

And when I came strolling in soon after, I was sporting the same blistering sunburn. Lou looked at Joe, and then he looked at me. And then it was almost like you could see the little light bulb go off over his head.

We were busted. Lou knew exactly where we had been that morning.

Joe quickly sneaked out of the clubhouse, and then Lou sat me down and let me know he was serious about the golf ban.

I got my one get-out-of-jail-free card, and I knew there wouldn't be another. So the golf clubs stayed at home. For real, this time.

THE BASTARD PLAY

Back in 1989 when Tommy Helms took over for Pete, we had this thing called a *bastard play*.

Here's how it worked. If there was a runner on first and you were thinking about sacrificing him over to second, you'd keep an eye on the third baseman. If he started charging toward home plate (which meant he had a good shot at getting to the ball quickly and throwing out the runner at second), you'd instead pull the bat back and give it a half-swing (a *slug bunt*) to try to knock a shot over his head.

In theory, it was a smart play. Unfortunately, Phil Garner, who was playing third base for Houston one time when I tried it, wasn't the type of player to be tricked so easily.

I started to bunt, but out of the corner of my eye, I saw Phil charging toward home. So I pulled back the bat and went for the slug bunt. Phil, though, had only faked charging in. So when I slapped the ball, he was in the perfect position to turn the double play.

The next time up, the same exact result. I slug-bunted into another double play after Phil faked me out. I was so embarrassed, and I got chewed out for getting duped twice. For years, I never considered using the bastard play again.

Well, on July 1, 1992, we were playing Houston again, and I came to the plate with Freddie Benavides on first. The bastard play made perfect sense because I knew Ken Caminiti, who was playing third base, would charge toward home plate.

Butch Henry fired the pitch, I squared to bunt, and sure enough, Caminiti came charging in. So I pulled back the bat and knocked a shot over Caminiti's head.

It worked to perfection. It was a double and scored Freddie from first.

After Reggie Sanders struck out, Hal Morris then lined a shot to center field. We were in the sixth inning, and the game was tied. Plus, there were two outs, so I knew I had to go for broke.

I shot around third base and charged for home. The throw was right on the money, so I slid, legs first. Unfortunately, right before I got to the plate, Scott Service turned his body and attempted to block the plate. My knee collided with his, and seeing how he had shin guards on, I took the brunt of the impact.

I knew it was bad right away. The pain crept in almost immediately. And then to add insult to injury, I heard home-plate umpire Ed Montague's call.

"Yerrrr out!"

Now I was really pissed.

Still lying on my back, I laid into Ed.

"Are you kidding me!?!? You idiot, I was safe by a mile! How in the hell can you call me out?"

Ed was covering his mouth, obviously trying to hide the fact that he was laughing.

"You wanna tell me what's so damn funny?" I asked.

"You," he said. "You can't argue with me. You can't even stand up!"

Ed had a point, and if it weren't for the unbelievable pain throbbing throughout my left knee, I probably would have been laughing, too.

But something was wrong. Really wrong, and I knew I'd soon be on the disabled list for the first time in my career.

BAD MEDICINE

After the collision, I tried to be a tough guy and walked off the field toward the clubhouse. As I politely tipped my cap to the few cheers, I was cursing under my breath and ready to pass out from the pain.

Once in the clubhouse, our trainer, Larry Starr, tried to move around a few things. I screamed in pain. I felt like I could have thrown up because it just hurt so damn badly.

They said I had torn up my knee in two places, and the ligament damage was substantial.

I flew home a day later and made an appointment with the team doctor. I showered that morning, and sadly, I got stuck in the tub. I couldn't lift my leg high enough to get out of it. When I tried, the pain was horrendous.

But I finally made it to our team doctor, and within an hour of seeing me, he had me in a cast up to my hip. My toes were turned and pointed back toward my body. It was so uncomfortable, and he said I was going to have to stay like that for six months.

When I woke up the next morning, I was in crippling pain. I called my neighbor and told him to bring a saw. I couldn't stay in that position. The doctor had to have screwed something up, I thought.

Luckily, my agent had been on the phone during this time trying to locate the best doctor he could find to look at my knee. He eventually tracked down Richard Steadman, the head doctor of the U.S. Olympic ski team, in Colorado. We met with him, and instead of that big gaudy cast, he fitted me in a light brace after he performed surgery. The brace felt a million times better, and it even let me work on building some strength in my leg despite the injury.

I returned to Cincinnati soon after, and the team doctor said he wanted to look at the knee. My stitches weren't due out for another week, but he insisted they were ready. He pulled them out, and I began bleeding immediately.

"That's the last time that quack ever touches me," I told Larry.

It's bad enough when you have to go through a serious injury for the first time, but when you have no confidence in the guy who's supposed to be looking over you, you can't help but fear the worst.

PAYROLL BANDITS

They said I'd be out until at least the following season after my knee injury, and I hated it.

I didn't know what to do. I was a pretty active person, but the disabled list was completely foreign territory to me. All of the sudden, I was immobile and helpless.

I dropped by the ballpark when the team was in town, but it wasn't the same.

I hated being a *payroll bandit*, as I called it. It was a term we used to describe guys collecting paychecks while contributing nothing to the team. Some guys were proud to be payroll bandits. They wouldn't go on the disabled list, but they refused to play. They just screwed around, sat on the bench, and collected their paychecks while claiming they had some phantom injury.

I had a legitimate excuse for not playing, but I felt like a bandit anyway. I hated being in the clubhouse and getting those looks of sympathy and those gratuitous pats on the back. After all, I was a living, breathing example of how playing a simple game can have real consequences. Guys can't play 100 percent if they've got paranoia about getting injured in their back of their minds. And walking around on a pair of crutches in front of my teammates made them acknowledge it.

It's just such a horrible feeling for a guy to have—that he's actually hurting his teammates simply by being around them.

I made my trips to the ballpark as infrequently as possible to avoid it. It was tough, but I felt it was best for my own sanity and the sanity of my teammates. I just felt so out of place—in a clubhouse I had always considered a second home. And to top it off, I was getting paid handsomely for it.

How could you not feel like a bandit?

FEELING UP TO PAR

I was counting down the days until that brace came off. I just couldn't wait.

While the rest of the 1992 season concluded without me, I just concentrated on my knee.

On the day before I was scheduled to go brace-less, I called the doctor's assistant and asked if it would be all right to take it off a day early. I got the go-ahead, so long as I promised I would be careful and take it easy.

I think I stayed up the whole night cleaning the basement, sweeping the floors, and going up and down the stairs. The sooner I got back into my old ways, I thought, the sooner I'd be back on the mound in uniform. Looking back, it was pretty stupid, but when you're cooped up inside all day for months on end, you just can't help yourself.

The next day I hobbled into the kitchen and told my wife I was going to run out and do some errands.

"Just take it easy," Deb pleaded.

And I did take it easy—on the golf course. I grabbed my clubs and played 18 holes. I was stiff as a board and couldn't really bend my knee the whole way, but I had never been happier to be on the course.

When I came home, I had a sheepish grin on my face.

"You played golf, didn't you?" Deb asked.

I could never get away with anything with her.

"Yeah, I did," I admitted.

Deb just shook her head.

"You're such an idiot, Tom."

THE B.I.P. AWARD

After I injured my knee during the 1992 season, Tim Belcher called me at home to tell me I had missed one of the year's great award ceremonies. Apparently, the team had finally found a recipient worthy of the Body in Pain Award—The B.I.P. Award, as they called it.

Prior to the season, the Reds dealt Randy Myers to San Diego for Bip Roberts. Bip was a good player, but he complained pretty often about every single injury and ailment he was suffering from or thought he was suffering from.

Nobody wants to poke fun at someone else's misfortunes, but it was hard not to laugh when he explained he had a bone chip in one of his shoulders. "I have a chip on my shoulder," he used to say. I don't think he ever understood why we thought that line was so funny.

Bip probably had one of his best seasons in 1992, hitting .323 with 44 stolen bases. He even tied a National League record in September by getting a hit in 10 consecutive at-bats. But he continued to complain about all of his injuries. I think he wanted to make sure we knew how tough he was.

To make sure he understood we heard him loud and clear, Belcher went out and bought a trophy. He said it was huge, probably two or three feet tall, and had a plate with "The B.I.P. Award" inscribed on it.

They presented Bip with the award one day in the clubhouse. They said he was overwhelmed and almost choked up. I guess Bip realized we had finally gotten his message. Belcher was telling me the story over the phone, and we were cracking up. I couldn't believe I missed that ceremony.

Even today, Bip remains the only recipient of the prestigious B.I.P. Award.

MOW WITH A PRO

During one of my visits to the stadium at the end of the 1992 season, I finally saw the conclusion of a prank two months in the making.

Earlier that year, we found an ad in a magazine that Paul O'Neill did for John Deere. Paul was sitting on a tractor, and his wife was standing next to him holding their first kid, who was about a year or two old. The headline was "Mow with a Pro."

Chris Sabo was always an instigator back then, so there was no way Paul was going to get away with something like that.

Sabes took a photo of Marge, cut out the head, and placed it over Paul's wife's head. He then did the same thing with Lou's picture and put it over the baby's head.

Paul, Marge, and Lou—what a happy-looking family.

Sabes then took the ad and hung it next to the water cooler in the lounge. It hung there for a month or two before Lou finally noticed it one day. We were sitting at a table, and we saw Lou walk by. He stopped, did a double-take, and then walked right up to the ad and squinted to see if he was seeing what he thought he was.

We all start snickering as Lou just stood there staring at the picture.

He finally just shook his head and walked out of the clubhouse.

Apparently, the thought of being Marge's offspring was just too much for him to handle.

THRILLA NAMED PINIELLA

As it turned out, Lou's final season in Cincinnati was 1992. Despite the team's unimaginable success (he won 90 games despite using mostly a

Class AAA team because of so many injuries), Marge just wasn't showing him much appreciation.

Earlier in the year, umpire Gary Darling got the Major League Umpires Association to file a $5 million lawsuit against Lou after he clamed Gary was biased against the Reds. Gary had a history of making calls against the Reds, and I think Lou was just fed up. Unfortunately, the Reds didn't help Lou at all, and he was left to fight the suit on his own.

Additionally, there was no talk of renewing Lou's contract, despite his success with the club.

I think it all just came to a head in September that year.

I don't remember the particulars, but Rob Dibble had said something to Lou about getting a night off if possible because his arm was aching. After the game, the writers spoke to Lou, and then to Dibs, and then to Lou again. Somehow, the stories didn't match up or the writers were just trying to instigate something. They'd run to Lou's office, and then to Dibs at his locker, and then back to Lou's office, each time relaying what the other was saying. Apparently, something set off Lou.

He came storming out of his office and decked Dibs. He just tackled him and wrestled him to the floor.

I was in the back of the clubhouse and just thought, "You gotta be kidding me."

Basically, you had two hard-headed bully-types clashing. Neither one was used to backing down from anything, and I think they both were just stressed and ready to explode at any moment.

I remember everyone trying to break the two of them up. Barry Larkin, who had just gotten out of the shower, was trying to hold both of them back with one arm while trying to keep his towel up with the other. Tim Belcher was trying to distract a camera guy who was taping the whole thing, and it felt like all hell had broken loose in our little clubhouse.

We eventually separated the two of them, but the damage had been done. It was the proverbial nail in Lou's coffin.

I heard that they did, in fact, offer Lou a contract at the end of the season, but they actually requested that he take a pay cut. Lou obviously declined the contract and said he was leaving.

I was devastated. Although I had butted heads a few times myself with Lou, I knew he was the best manager I'd ever have. I knew how lucky we were to have him, and I was crushed knowing that his time with the Reds was over.

The only thing that took the sting away was learning who our next skipper was going to be.

BAD OMEN

About a month after the season, we got the news that Tony Perez was taking over the helm of the Reds.

Since joining the club in 1984, I always thought that Tony was one of the premiere veterans who made me appreciate being in the Reds clubhouse. You just can't have enough guys like him around. He's just what the younger guys need.

Although I was saddened to see Lou go, Tony was the greatest replacement I could have asked for.

But I should have been skeptical when Jim Bowden, the Reds new general manager, didn't let Tony hire any of his own coaches (other than Dave Bristol).

Usually, a manager gets to name his own staff, but Tony was given no such luxury. It seemed so odd.

Regardless, I was stoked to get my knee healthy and get to camp. I just couldn't wait to play for Tony.

MEAN GENE

I received medical clearance in January that my reconstructed knee was ready for spring training.

I never doubted that it would be, but it was definitely comforting to know that my knee responded well to every test they threw at it. I would have to wear a brace early on, but it was a small price to pay to be back on the mound.

Once I got to camp, Tony said he wasn't going to worry about me. He told me that he understood that I knew what I needed to do to get ready for the season. He also told the front office that.

Apparently, though, it fell on deaf ears.

I was throwing on the side during one of our first sessions in camp, and Gene Bennett, one of Jim's advisers, came up behind the plate with a radar gun. I usually liked Gene. He seemed like a good guy, a "baseball guy."

But once I saw the gun, I was ticked. That gun wasn't going to tell him anything that we didn't already know. It was way too early in camp to start worrying about my velocity. I hadn't even had a chance to get my legs under me.

Very matter-of-factly, I warned him.

"Gene, get out of my way," I said, "or I'm going to hit you in the head with this next pitch."

Gene didn't say a word and just walked off. And no one came near me with a radar gun for the rest of the spring.

BULLETS OVER SAN DIEGO

One of our new arrivals in 1993 was Kevin Mitchell.

Mitchell had won the 1989 National League MVP Award with the Giants, but injuries were becoming a problem.

Still, though, he was considered one of the league's great power hitters, and I think Jim Bowden easily fell in love with big home-run hitters like him.

One day in the clubhouse, Mitchell was changing, and I saw a big round scar on his back.

"What's that?" I asked.

"Bullet wound," he said.

"A bullet wound?" I asked, intrigued.

"Yeah, a bullet wound. Drive by."

"A drive by?" I asked, now astonished. "Were they trying to shoot you?"

"Nope. Some other dude."

"Well, did they apologize?" I asked, actually being serious.

Mitchell looked at me like I had two heads growing out of my neck.

"Man, bullets ain't got no name on them!"

Apparently, he had walked a few miles after he had been shot, a bullet still lodged in him, before he made it home and collapsed.

A few months after he told me about getting shot, Mitchell took a few of the guys from the clubhouse back to his old stomping grounds when we were in town to play the Padres. And once again, bullets were flying. Apparently, one of our star teammates nearly got capped.

And that was the last time anyone wanted to find out more about Mitchell's old neighborhood.

HIRED TO BE FIRED

He was hired to be fired. No doubt about it.

Just 44 games into the 1993 season, and just four games under .500, Tony was axed in the cruelest treatment of a person I had ever seen during my decade in the major leagues.

A Cincinnati institution, a Big Red Machine hero, and the leader of our squad—thrown out like yesterday's garbage.

It was sickening. Never had I been so upset and so disappointed in an organization I once adored.

But Tony was part of the old regime, and team management was undergoing a transformation under Jim Bowden.

Yes, we were infuriated by the treatment of Tony, but more than anything, we were completely blindsided. Who in the hell fires a manager after 44 games—especially when they're just four games under?

God, I still get pissed just thinking about it.

Do you know how Tony found out? They called him by phone. A guy who spent the majority of his adult life doing everything he could for the club, and they dismiss him with a simple phone call.

There was another aspect of the whole situation that irked me. Prior to Tony's hiring, Marge was being lambasted for supposed racial and ethnic remarks she had made. Was Tony's hiring simply a Band-Aid to make people forget?

We will never know.

One thing we do know was that all of the guys in the clubhouse could find little reason to trust anything management had to say to us.

After Tony's firing, Bowden called a meeting in the clubhouse and tried to express his sympathy for us losing our manager, and he assured us things would improve. But by that time, no one could believe anything we were told.

It was one of the few times in my career I was embarrassed to wear a Cincinnati uniform.

UP ON THE ROOF

If I had never thrown a perfect game, surely my lasting legacy as a ballplayer would have been my memorable day in Chicago on July 7, 1993.

Here's how it happened.

I had heard that Bob Walk, a pitcher with Pittsburgh, had got into the scoreboard at Wrigley Field. It was old school, and people still changed the scores and the pitch counts and everything by hand, so there was plenty of room to walk around in there. So I wanted to know if I could get in there to check it, seeing how I wasn't pitching that day. But they wouldn't let me.

So I went into the clubhouse and talked to Tom Hellman, the visiting clubhouse manager in Chicago, and asked if he knew anyone who owned any of the buildings that overlooked the ballpark in the outfield.

"Yeah, a guy named George," he said. "He owns a few of them, I think."

We got George on the phone, and I explained that I wanted to sit on one of his buildings for an inning.

"Well, that sounds like fun," he said. "Meet me at Murphy's Pub in the top of the third inning."

I was sitting in the bullpen, and once we got to the second inning, I stood up.

"Well fellas, keep an eye out for me," I said.

Then they asked where I was going.

"Don't worry," I assured them. "You'll find me."

I went upstairs to the clubhouse, threw a black sweat suit over my uniform, and exited the stadium.

I met George in the bar, we walked a few blocks to the building, and then we went up three flights of stairs to the roof.

There was a party going on. The place was packed with people, the grill was going, and everyone had a beer.

I took off the sweat suit, sat down, and let my feet dangle over the edge of the building. I then took off my cap and started waving it. One by one, the fans and my teammates started to notice. Belcher, wanting to know if he was really seeing what he thought he was, got one of the cameramen to zoom in on me, and that's when I was busted, as I would later find out.

While I was on the roof, Kevin Mitchell hit his second home run of the game, putting us ahead for good. I felt like maybe my little trip brought some luck to the team. We had been struggling, so I considered staying up there an extra inning or two. But then I thought better of the idea and said my goodbyes to the Cubs fans.

Here is the proof that I was indeed on the roof overlooking Wrigley.

I was back in the dugout by the fourth inning and received some pats on the back. I then settled in to watch the rest of the game (which included Jose Rijo squirting some old ladies with a Super Soaker and chasing them out of their seats—it was just a crazy game).

By the end of the game, I had pretty much forgotten about the whole roof thing until a reporter came up to ask me about it. Before I could even answer, Davey Johnson, our manager who was brought in to replace Tony, tapped me on the shoulder and said he wanted to see me in his office.

I had successfully pulled off one of the game's greatest pranks, but I was now going to pay the price for it.

ROOF COLLAPSE

Davey obviously wasn't thrilled about my leaving the park, and he explained that sitting on a roof like that could have resulted in an injury or worse. Even though I was pretty safe and there was a landing just a few feet underneath in case I did fall, I let Davey continue on.

I knew he was probably just upset because he thought I was showing him up. After he finished with his little speech, I responded.

"Look, first of all, this has nothing to do with you," I said. "I did it for those guys out there, the guys in that clubhouse. Since Tony's been fired, we've had 25 guys going in 25 different directions. I just wanted to do something to lighten the mood and bring everyone back together.

"So please don't personalize it. It really had nothing to do with you. I know that leaving the stadium in my uniform was wrong. But that's the only thing. I don't regret anything else. Just fine me or whatever you have to do."

And he did, $1,000, which had to be paid to his wife's charity.

But that was the end of it. Everyone got a good laugh out of it, and that's all I wanted all along.

LEGACY OF THE ROOF

I should have known that my roof excursion wouldn't simply go away. Even today, I'm asked about it all the time.

I ended up making national headlines, and replays of me sitting on top of the roof flashed across news stations all over the country in the days that followed. The whole thing took on a life all its own.

Later that season when we headed south to play the Florida Marlins, their CEO, Wayne Huizenga, asked me if I'd spend an inning sitting in his center field restaurant during the game. Every time I returned to Chicago, I had invites to join fans on the roofs. I must have gotten a million requests and invitations like that. But I had to turn down every one. It was absolutely a one-time thing.

Although I'm a little embarrassed about the monster I created, I don't regret what I did. After all, I accomplished everything I wanted to. The guys got a good laugh out of it, and for the first time in a long time, we felt some team unity. Sometimes laughter really is the best medicine.

Because all of us were so upset about losing Tony, I know a lot of people think that I went on the roof just to show up team management. But that's just not true. I've never been much of a troublemaker. I've never been the type to try to show up my manager or coaches. Hell, it was in the Reds' own farm system that I learned not to do stuff like that.

I just took my role as a veteran and leader seriously back then. We were stuck in a funk, and we were too disjointed to be a team. Something needed to be done, and climbing on that roof was the best thing I could think of.

DL'D AGAIN

I thought things were bad enough in 1993, but then they got worse. In August, I managed to land myself on the disabled list once again.

We were playing the Dodgers in Los Angeles, and Raul Mondesi was at bat. We had a runner on first, so when Mondesi hit a one-hopper back to me, I was determined to get the double play.

I put down my glove and my other hand to try to corral the ball, but it bounced up and hit the middle finger on my pitching hand. Something was wrong because the tip of my finger instantly felt like it was burning. I hesitated for a second and then threw to first to get just the one out.

I tried to pitch to the next batter, but the tip of my finger felt like it was three times the size. It felt like it was on fire and was just throbbing.

I left the game soon after, and the Dodgers' team doctor did an X-ray and confirmed I had chipped the bone at the tip of my finger.

Obviously, I was discouraged, but I committed myself to getting back into the rotation before the end of the season. After about three weeks, I was feeling good.

Davey Johnson, though, didn't want to hear any of it. Despite pitching my normal side session and feeling no discomfort, Davey insisted that something was "off."

He then told me to pitch with my arm stretched out more. It was a completely different follow-through than I had used my entire career, but if it meant getting me back in the rotation, I figured I'd give it a shot.

I threw one pitch, and I felt a sharp jolt in the bone of my left arm, right under the bicep muscle. It hurt terribly, and I knew something was wrong. As it turned out, that pain came in the exact spot where I'd break my arm a year later. I still wonder if that weird throwing motion caused a stress fracture.

I never did pitch again in 1993. And as it turned out, the following season would be my last in Cincinnati.

ONE-SIDED CONVERSATION

Leave it to Chris Sabo to get ejected for talking to himself.

We were playing the Dodgers in Los Angeles, and after being called out on strikes, Sabes went out to the field to play third base. He was still fuming about the call, though, and kept muttering to himself.

Eventually, third-base umpire Larry Vanover called time. He then told Sabes to knock it off.

Sabes kept muttering, though, and Vanover soon had enough.

He gave him the boot, which didn't go over well. Sabes just couldn't understand how he was tossed for talking to no one but himself.

"F---, I wasn't even cussin'!" Sabo said on his way to the clubhouse.

A DOPEY MISTAKE

The 1993 season was one of my worst—with the finger injury, the firing of Tony, and the overall collapse of team morale.

But during the second week of August, my career suffered a real black eye, one that still follows me today.

I was racing back home after a golf outing so I could get to my son's sixth birthday party. I stopped off at the convenience store near our house for a can of Copenhagen, and while there, I saw two buddies who were obviously in no shape to drive. They asked if I could give them a ride home. It wasn't too far out of my way, so I didn't mind.

While in my truck, one of them asked if he could light up. Once he pulled an odd-looking cigarette out of his pocket, I realized it wasn't a cigarette at all. It was a joint. I don't know why I didn't stop them right there, but I didn't, and I regret it.

I dropped them off and then headed for home. Traffic was backed up on I-275, but I was really close to my exit, so I took the shoulder for the eighth-mile or so that was left before I got to the exit.

I passed a cop, though, and he flipped on his lights and pulled up behind me. Once he got to my truck, he could smell the odor of marijuana and asked if I had been smoking. I assured him I hadn't. He believed me because he could tell I had my wits about me. But they brought in a dog to sniff around the truck, and they found the remnant of the joint one of those idiots left in the ashtray.

I was then arrested for possession of marijuana.

News of the arrest quickly spread throughout Cincinnati, and I was vilified by many people. I was made out to be a druggie, even when I explained that the pot wasn't mine.

I had made a mistake, but I hadn't smoked anything in my truck.

And as it turned out, a drug test that I took after the arrest proved my innocence. Unfortunately, the fact that I hadn't been doing drugs was picked up by only a few media outlets. Even today, I think the majority of Reds fans never realized the pot wasn't mine.

No matter. I think a lot of the damage had already been done. However, I knew I only had myself to blame. It wasn't my pot and I hadn't smoked it, but I was just as stupid for having allowed it in my truck. And the possession charge stuck.

During the entire thing, I maintained I was innocent without going into detail about what had happened. I didn't want to get anyone else in trouble, and besides, I knew I was just as much at fault for permitting those guys to smoke it in my truck.

There are very few things I regret in my career, and that's the biggest. I really hurt my reputation, and I let down a lot of fans. That was the hardest part of the whole thing. I didn't mind the fine or the community service; I just regretted giving people who once supported me a reason to think twice about my character. That hurt more than anything.

PROVING MY WORTH

Even in 1994, which was going to be my 11th season in the majors, I went to camp feeling like I had something to prove. I felt like I still had to earn a spot in the rotation, even though I was probably a lock simply because they were paying me so much.

I knew that management probably wasn't going to stick one of their highest-paid starting pitchers into the bullpen, but after suffering season-ending injuries in 1992 and 1993, I figured I needed to really show them something in camp in 1994.

And after the rooftop incident and the arrest the year before, I knew I needed to remind everyone that I wasn't a delinquent or a distraction.

I vowed that 1994 would strictly be about pitching and winning ballgames for the team.

Unfortunately, I would soon be making national headlines once again.

FIRST HINT OF PAIN

I pitched the third game of the season in 1994. But I was given just a half-hour notice that I'd be filling in for Erik Hanson, who claimed he was too sick to start—30 minutes before game time. I was used to preparing all day for a start, but we didn't really have any alternatives, so I sucked it up and went out there—and got rocked.

But I bounced back. The team started winning some games, and after that rough season debut against the Cardinals, I went 3-0 in my next four starts.

After throwing back-to-back complete games, we headed down to Florida toward the end of April. I pitched the series opener, but as the game wore on, my arm started to ache more and more. Right under my shoulder on my pitching arm—it was just a constant, piercing pain.

We headed to Chicago soon afterward, and I went running with Rick Stowe, our clubhouse guy. As we ran along Lake Michigan, I remember the pain in my arm throbbing once again.

I stopped and began massaging my arm as deeply as I could.

"What's up?" Rick asked.

"Man, my arm is killing me," I said. "Just killing me."

Rick realized it wasn't just a normal ache.

"Right here, man, right here!" I said, as I grit my teeth and grimaced with pain. I could pinpoint the exact location where it was coming from.

I'll never forget that pain. It wasn't like a muscle strain or a bruise or anything. It was just a deep, sharp shooting pain that radiated out from the center of the bone.

Once we left Chicago and headed to San Diego, I'd learn exactly why the pain was so bad.

CRACK HEARD ROUND THE WORLD

Before my scheduled start against the Padres, I was trying anything to get my arm loose and pain free. I took some blood thinners hoping it would help, but obviously, all it did was make my arm weaker. I went under the riser seats and hung there, trying to stretch my arm out. Nothing seemed to work.

Regardless, I knew I had to pitch, so I took the mound.

It was May 9, 1994.

The pain was still there, but I was getting outs. I wasn't throwing any harder than probably 77 miles per hour, but hell, I think I took a perfect game into the sixth inning before I finally gave up a home run.

Still in that inning, I had men on second and third, and I had worked the count to two strikes on Archi Cianfrocco.

"Just reach back," I said to myself. "Reach back, get a little extra on this pitch, and get out of this mess."

I reared back, got some torque, and then I thrust my arm toward home plate.

What followed was the most God-awful cracking sound I had ever heard. It sounded like a whip cracking, and it echoed through Jack Murphy Stadium, as I would learn later, all the way up to the press box.

I lay on the ground, and I thought I had been shot. I thought my arm was blown clear off my body. I couldn't feel it.

"My arm's gone," I thought. "My damn arm is gone!"

Barry Larkin was the first guy to run over to me. I never had seen him look so pale. He softly put his hands on me as he tried to find something to say.

"Barry, is my arm still there?" I asked, probably on the verge of shock. "My arm, man, is it there?"

"Yeah, it's there, buddy," he said.

Well, I hadn't been shot. But I knew something serious had happened. The pain in my arm, the cracking sound, the ball flying off course—my God, I broke my arm. I broke my arm. My left arm—my pitching arm.

I then asked the next logical question.

"Lark, did any of those runs score?"

When my arm snapped mid-pitch, the ball careened toward the on-deck circle. It was the last thing I saw before I hit the ground in pain.

"Yeah," Barry said. "I think they both did. Sorry, man."

DEADLY HUMOR

They brought out a stretcher to get me off the field.

And if you thought I sweated profusely on a normal day, you can imagine the flood of sweat gushing out of my pores after breaking my arm.

Tim Pugh came running up to me as I was carried off the field, and he had a real look of panic on his face.

I slowly closed my eyes, and my face went blank.

"Tom! Man, Tom!" Timmy shouted. "Wake up! Wake up, Tom!"

He must have thought I was dying.

I quickly opened my eyes and gave him a wink.

"I'm just f----- with you," I said in between laughs and cries. "I'm here."

Even with a broken arm, I couldn't resist screwing with a teammate.

A DIP FOR A DIP

I ended up spending the night at Scripps Memorial Hospital in San Diego waiting to hear the status of my arm.

After a game, no matter if I pitched well or like crap, I always put in a big dip. It was a dirty habit I had picked up, but even with that broken arm, I needed a dip. I never did it while I was pitching, only after. And I was craving it by that time.

I was waiting to get X-rayed, and I saw the doctor. I asked him if it would be okay, and he reluctantly agreed.

They had my arms wrapped tightly to my body by that time so I wouldn't move and shift any bones. But once they were ready for X-rays, they unwrapped me, and I could feel the bones moving. My Copenhagen soon had a nauseating effect.

"He's going white," one of the nurses yelled. She must have thought I was ready to pass out or die. Nope. I was going to puke.

"No, I'm not going white," I assured them. "I just need to get this dip out, and now!"

THINKING OF DRAVECKY

I stayed awake that whole night. In my room, the TV was tuned to CNN *Headline News*, and they replayed the clip of me breaking my arm every 20 minutes—again and again and again.

I must have seen my arm snap a dozen times that night.

As sickening as it was, I was much happier to be watching it than going through it again.

Unfortunately, I had to wait all night for the primary doctor to arrive so we could figure out what to do about my arm. I had plenty of time for my mind to wander.

I remembered Dave Dravecky, a former major league pitcher who found a cancerous tumor in his pitching arm. After it was treated, he battled his way back to the bigs and even beat us in his return. It was such an inspirational event. But a few games later, he too snapped his arm while delivering a pitch.

I started to seriously consider the possibility that I had cancer and that was why my arm snapped like Dravecky's.

I thought about that all night, worried to death how I was going to explain to my family that I had cancer. It was a horrible feeling, a helpless feeling.

However, once the doctor got to the hospital and checked over everything, he put my mind at ease.

"It's not cancer," he said. "It's definitely not. Don't worry about that. It's nothing even close to Dravecky. This is completely different. It's a spiral oblique fracture."

It was just a huge, huge relief. I looked out the window and toward the sky and said a little prayer. My hospital bed overlooked a golf course, and as I looked out at it, I remembered something I had scheduled.

"Doc, I had an 8 a.m. tee time today," I said.

"Well, Tom," he said. "I seriously doubt you're going to make it."

STRUCK OUT

The doctor and I talked about the options for fixing my arm, and he mentioned the idea of plates and rods and screws and all types of other hardware.

"I'm going to look like a robot when they're finished with me!" I thought.

I feared that things could too easily go wrong doing any of that, and seeing how I wanted to pitch again, we eventually opted for a "hanging cast," which was weighted at the bottom of it so that it would pull your bone downward and straighten it out.

I slept in a recliner for three weeks after that. I couldn't lie on my back. It was horrible. I felt like a zombie. No one can get a good night's rest like that, but it was the only way to keep the bone from shifting.

They obviously stuck me on the disabled list during this time, but unfortunately, baseball went on strike. The rest of the season was cancelled.

It was my 10th year in the bigs, and after 10 years, you're supposed to be fully vested in the MLB pension. During the negotiations after the strike, however, they decided that guys on the 60-day disabled list didn't get credit.

I was now just a few months short of that pension, which any player will tell you, is what any veteran player is shooting for. It's a great pension, and if you can get the time to qualify, you're pretty much set for the rest of your life.

Whether I thought I'd really be ready or not, I knew I needed one more season in the majors.

SIGN OF THE TIMES

After I broke my arm, even the smallest of tasks became frustrating because of that huge cast.

Once I was back home, I went to one of my son's baseball games, and a guy recognized me and asked me for an autograph.

I looked at him, then at the pen, and then at my arm wrapped in a cast.

"I don't think it's possible," I said, tapping my arm.

It was a legitimate excuse, but it did little good.

"Well, can't you sign it with your other hand?" he asked.

Unbelievably, the guy was serious, and I knew he wouldn't take no for an answer. So I scribbled my name with my right hand. It wasn't even legible, but he didn't seem to care.

"Wow, thanks man," he said.

Luckily, I caught myself right before I said, "No problem."

WHY IT HAPPENED

After speaking with experts throughout the country, I started to piece together what went wrong with my arm.

Here's how I understand it.

After pitching well over 200 innings for years, I had built up some real strength and density in the bones of my pitching arm. I was using it so much, my bones naturally compensated by thickening.

It happens to everyone. My doctors said that the X-ray and bone density of a 16-year-old Roger Clemens wouldn't look anything like that of a 40-year-old Clemens. As your bones are used more and more, they become bigger and stronger.

However, after I hurt my knee in 1992 and my finger in 1993, my workload dropped substantially. I wasn't stressing the bone in my pitching arm like I usually did, and gradually, it shrunk back to its normal size.

So when I came out of the gates in 1994, including those back-to-back complete games, I went right back to pitching like I always had. Unfortunately, my bone didn't have the same density, and the stress I put on it was more than it could handle.

I had no idea my body wasn't ready for the workload, and more than likely, I developed a stress fracture as I pushed it too hard. That was the pain I had been feeling during the weeks before I broke my arm.

And it actually probably first developed in 1993 when Davey Johnson had me working out in the bullpen after that finger injury. My bone just didn't have the strength to handle what I was throwing at it.

Remember how I was able to pinpoint exactly where the pain was coming from? The doctors said that's a sign of something seriously wrong. Even today when I'm speaking to Little Leaguers and high school and college players, I encourage them to speak up if they ever feel that kind of pain.

Unfortunately, I just had no idea at the time.

SCABBED OVER

Because I hadn't reached any of the levels to kick in my option year for 1995, I was a free agent.

Obviously, most people probably thought I was damaged goods and wanted nothing to do with me. However, I figured that the Reds, the only major league team I had ever known, could find a spot for me. I wouldn't even want much in return. I just needed the service time for the pension, and I wanted at least to go out on my own terms.

My agent made a call to the club, and they said there was only one way I could come back—as a replacement player. It was the ultimate insult. There was no way I was going to be a scab, especially on a team that I had been a part of for more than a decade.

It was a horrible time in my career. The Reds obviously had no use for me, for whatever reasons. They didn't necessarily owe me anything, but I figured I had at least earned one final shot. I didn't even get that.

Honestly, I was pretty bitter, but I knew there was nothing I could do about it. So I just focused on getting ready for the season, wherever that might be.

The physical therapy that winter was brutal. They beat the crap out of me to get me back in shape. It's just what I needed, but it didn't keep me from crying every day that winter. It was just so intense and tiring, and I wanted to throw in the towel more than a few times.

I eventually landed in the Puerto Rican winter leagues that December. I knew I needed to pitch somewhere to see what I had, and when the opportunity presented itself, I took it. It was a crazy league, and I don't think I pitched until the playoffs, but I was effective. Not strong or dominating, but effective. And I never had a problem with my arm.

My persistence eventually paid off. Bob Boone, one of the Reds coaches when I broke my arm, got the manager's job in Kansas City, and he gave me an invite to spring training with them.

CAMP IN K.C.

Although I wanted to stay in baseball at almost any cost, I made sure my best interests were taken into consideration.

I would start off at Class AAA in 1995, but my contract said that I could look for work elsewhere if I wasn't called up after four starts.

Frankly, though, I was just happy to be pitching. I couldn't believe how quickly I was gone from Cincinnati. At first, it was a little strange going to camp with someone other than the Reds. Because of the designated hitter rule, I didn't take batting practice or bunt for the first time ever in camp. But pitching is pitching, and once I got back on the mound, my arm felt great, and I had all the confidence in the world.

However, once I made my first regular start down in Class AAA, all of the doubts and worries instantly came back.

I stood on the mound looking at the batter, and before I could even throw one pitch, I started worrying about breaking my arm again. It all came back. It was just a fearful moment and an eerie rush.

I went five innings, though, and I don't think I gave up a run or even a hit. I wasn't throwing hard, but well, I never threw very hard.

I had pitched well, but I just knew my head and heart weren't in it.

EARLY DEPARTURE

I think it was after my third start in Class AAA that I got called up to the Royals' major league team.

I made two starts. One was against the Angels and one against the A's.

I threw no harder than 80 miles per hour, and they were hitting me at will. I remember telling the trainer that I just wasn't feeling right.

They were running MRIs on me for two days, and then they eventually moved me to the disabled list. Soon after, I made a rehab assignment back down in Class AAA, and then I was scheduled to join the big league club in New York and pitch for the first time in Yankee Stadium.

My dad was a huge Yankees fan, so I arranged a flight and tickets for him.

Unfortunately, I never made it to New York.

In my last rehab start in Omaha, I felt something in my shoulder during the third inning. As it turned out, I hadn't prepared my shoulder or elbow properly. I spent all of that time strengthening my arm, but was oblivious to how weak those other small muscles had gotten. Physically, I just wasn't ready to be back in the majors.

I called the Royals general manager, Herk Robinson, that day and said I was going home. I told him he didn't even have to pay me. I told him my arm wasn't ready and that I would just focus on getting ready for 1996.

ONE LAST HURRAH

Instead of going home to sulk, I worked harder than I had ever worked before. The Royals had offered nothing more than a "maybe" when it came to starting for them in 1996, but that maybe was enough to keep me going. All day, every day, I busted my hump. All I needed was my arm to respond.

But it was all for naught.

I did end up going back to spring training with the Royals in 1996, and I had every intention of getting back to the majors. Unfortunately, my arm didn't have the same intentions.

It was March 24, 1996. My anniversary.

I pitched two or three innings, and I just didn't have it. I left the game and headed straight for the showers. I always stuck around in the dugout after I left a game, but on that day, the passion was gone.

I soaked in the shower for 20 or 30 minutes and finally accepted that it was over. Yeah, I probably could have hung around for another few years as a reliever, but working out of the bullpen never interested me. I was a starting pitcher. And if I couldn't be that, then baseball just didn't appeal to me.

I walked into Bob Boone's office. Greg Luzinski, George Brett, and a few other guys were in there.

"My grind's over," I told Bob.

I rambled on for another 20 minutes about how much I loved the game, how much I wanted to be a pitcher, and how much I appreciated the shot they gave me. But then I told them I needed to accept reality and acknowledge that my time was over.

"I had a great run, boys," I said, with tears still in my eyes. "But it's over."

We shook hands, and I said my goodbyes.

It was one of the saddest days of my life. Although I was able to get my full pension, professional baseball, the only thing I had ever known in my adult life, was no longer a part of me.

ALWAYS A RED

I guess I technically retired a Kansas City Royal, but my heart was always in Cincinnati.

When I left the game in 1996, I left without regrets. I failed in my comeback attempt, but at least I knew I could go through the rest of my life without thinking, "What if?"

But there was a hole in my heart when it was all over. I missed the major league lifestyle, but I also missed all the little things: the thrill of pitching in front of a crowd, feeling a part of something bigger than myself, and most importantly, watching the game with my teammates from a little spot in the dugout. I missed it all terribly.

I also missed being a Cincinnati Red. No one will ever know how much the organization means to me. It's a part of me, and I'm more proud of being associated with the club than just about anything else in my life.

WINNING BY LOSING

Throughout my life, I've always remembered one of my favorite quotes from former golfer Ben Hogan. He said something like, "I've never learned anything from winning."

What he was saying is that it's not during the good times that you gain any real knowledge. You learn valuable lessons from tough times, when things aren't going your way. In the face of adversity is when you learn what you're made of, what it takes to compete, and how to push yourself to the extremes.

Getting to the major leagues and having a fair amount of success never came easy for me. But as much as I learned getting there, the real lessons came after I suffered some serious setbacks, including all of those injuries toward the end of my career.

The great thing about playing baseball is that you can take everything you learn—camaraderie, teamwork, and personal responsibility—and use it for the rest of your life. That's why you see the great ones develop successful second careers in things like business, broadcasting and coaching. And that's why I was so thrilled when I was invited to Cincinnati's spring training as a special instructor in January 2006.

Dealing with injuries was just part of the education process for me.

I have no doubts in my mind that I'm a better person today because of those setbacks I faced toward the end of my career. It was hard to recognize it at the time, but in the past decade, I've used those lessons on a near-daily basis.

Am I happy I got injured? Of course not. I would have been quite happy to go through my entire career dodging injuries and playing into my 40s. However, because life threw me a few curveballs, I was able to learn more about myself and what it takes to succeed. I learned exactly what I'm capable of achieving and overcoming.

Honestly, I am guy who believes in fate. I believe people are destined for certain things. And I believe that in the grand scheme of things, I suffered those setbacks to help me become a better person.

I'm thankful for the opportunities I was given, the people I've met, and the places I've gone. I'm proud to be a Cincinnati Red and everything it entailed—the good and the bad.

12

LIFE AFTER BASEBALL

NO REGRETS

I spent 99 percent of my career in a Reds uniform. It would have been great to spend the whole thing in Cincinnati, but honestly, I feel a great sense of relief and pride for getting to spend any time at all with the organization, let alone 11 unforgettable seasons.

When you think about it, I really did overcome the odds. I grew up loving just one team, which just happened to be the team that drafted me, promoted me through its minor league system, and then allowed me to play on baseball's biggest stage with my childhood heroes.

It's tough to retire from the game, but when I look back at my career, I have nothing to regret. I was one of the lucky ones. I achieved accomplishments both personally and as a team, and I did it with the Cincinnati Reds, the organization that meant the most to me.

NUXHALL WINS

I don't think one person will ever mean as much to one organization as the "Ol' Left-hander" means to the Cincinnati Reds.

Joe Nuxhall is quite simply a Cincinnati icon. In a game where certain individuals mean different things to different generations, Nuxhall is the exception. He's the guy who bridges the gap between fans of all ages. No one has ever had that type of impact and never again will.

I knew I'd never be in Joe's class when it came to that type of mass appeal, but he was definitely a motivating force when it came to my pitching career. For as long as I pitched in Cincinnati, I wanted to top his Reds total of 130 wins. If I could beat his total, I knew I would have really "made it."

Each victory from 1984 to 1994 got me one step closer. Whenever I won a game, I always thought about how much closer I was getting to my good friend.

But when my career ended in 1995, I realized I fell short of my goal—by seven victories.

There's just no topping the Ol' Left-hander.

EVERYDAY PEOPLE

One of the greatest things I've learned about ballplayers is how down to earth most of them are. I've been around the game for more than 25 years now, and rarely have I met someone from the game whose ego is so big you can't get to know him as a real person.

Most guys who become major leaguers—even your bona fide superstars—were usually just kids who found baseball as a way to prove their worth.

They're guys who found baseball as an outlet and channeled all of their energy toward the game. They're not superior people. In fact, I think some of them may even be inferior in some ways. I'm guessing a lot of misfits found baseball as their way to productive and meaningful lives.

I'm sure that 99 percent of major leaguers are just average, regular guys. We just happen to have a specific talent that translates well to professional sports.

Eddie Murray is a perfect example. I held the guy up on a pedestal, but when I finally met him at the 1991 All-Star Game, I realized he was just a normal guy who didn't consider himself better than anyone else. He saw everyone as being on the same level as him. He was wise enough to know that a person shouldn't be judged by his statistics alone.

During my years with the Reds and the years after my retirement, I've tried to model myself after guys like Eddie. I understand that I was lucky to have the talents I did. That's why even today I try to stay involved with the Reds community and make myself approachable to fans. It's important that they know that we're normal people who really appreciate the support we receive.

Besides, at the end of the day, I'm a Reds fan just like everyone else. Talking about the Reds isn't a job or a chore. It's something I love and am lucky to have been a part of for so long. I'm happy to share it with anyone who will listen.

FOR PETE'S SAKE

At the end of the 2002 baseball season, I was invited back to Cinergy Field with many of my former teammates for the stadium's closing ceremonies. With Great American Ball Park nearly built, Cinergy was slated for an implosion. We got one last chance to rekindle all those great memories.

One by one, we were announced and took our spots along the foul lines. We wore our old jerseys and tipped our caps to the crowd one last time. Every great memory of my career came rushing back.

Dozens and dozens of us were introduced. And then, to close out the introductions, they brought out all of the Reds legends—Johnny Bench, Joe Morgan, Tony Perez, and those guys. But as each was introduced, the grumblings got louder and louder for Pete Rose, who wasn't allowed to attend the ceremonies because of his banishment from baseball.

I knew the fans wanted Pete to get the recognition he deserved, so I ran into the tunnel under the stadium to find a can of spray paint. A stadium worker eventually located a red can, and I headed out to the pitcher's mound and laid down some long red lines to make a perfect "14," the unmistakable uniform number of Pete.

The fans cheered as though Pete were there in person. Pete needed to be acknowledged, and I was just happy the opportunity presented itself.

I think it was a fitting salute. After all, it was Pete who taught me that if something needed to be said, you were usually better off just saying it.

Pete meant a lot to the city and the fans, and that day, something needed to be said to acknowledge it.

The ceremonies went on without him, but it felt good to do him right.

I'm introduced to the crowd during closing ceremonies at Cinergy Field in 2002.
Photo courtesy of the Cincinnati Reds

EXTRA INNINGS

After those closing ceremonies at Cinergy Field, we enjoyed one final hurrah at the old stadium.

Before it was blown to smithereens, the stadium played host to one final game—a softball game hosted by Pete Rose. As a non-Reds and non-Major League Baseball event, the game allowed Pete free rein one last time.

And Pete put together one hell of an event. Who else could get 42,000 people to come watch a bunch of old fat guys play some beer-league softball?

Pete put together a Reds alumni team, as well as a team made up of former major leaguers, including guys like Steve Carlton, Mike Schmidt, Gary Carter, and Ryne Sandberg.

The ultimate honor came when Pete named me the starting pitcher for the Reds team. I remember standing on the mound, hearing the packed house, and then like second nature, looking behind me to see who was going to take any throws at second. Joe Morgan gave his chest a tap, no doubt in baseball mode himself. It felt like old times.

The dugout felt just as familiar. We had the guys from the Big Red Machine—Pete, Joe, Johnny Bench, George Foster, and the others—and guys from my generation like Eric Davis, Dave Parker, and Ronnie Oester. We razzed each other nonstop. All of the Big Red Machine guys were badgering each other just like it was 1975 again.

A NEW LOVE

It's hard to go from such a competitive environment into the doldrums of retirement. As much as I loved having the extra time with my family, I needed something to fill the void of baseball.

For me, that was golf.

Some of my favorite memories from my playing days took place on the golf course. From Joe Nuxhall getting his club stuck in a tree after a horrible tee shot—and spending half an hour trying to get it back down—to watching Tom Glavine and Greg Maddux run from black snakes on the Traditions Golf Course like they were king cobras.

After I recovered from my broken arm in 1994, my golf mechanics really improved, and with baseball no longer occupying my time, I was hitting the links almost every day. I loved the competition. I also loved that no matter how fat my old teammates and I got, we could still golf and get better.

I got serious about the game and had some real success. I was a scratch golfer and started making a name for myself in some of the area golf tournaments.

To stay on top of my game, though, would have required a real time commitment, one that I wasn't willing to make with my kids entering school and their own sports. My priorities at home came first, so golf now remains just a hobby.

I think the competitive juices will always be in me. Baseball engrains it in you, and it's a good thing.

So if you ever see me on the links, feel free to say hello. I'd love to talk about Reds baseball and even hear about your favorite memory from when I was pitching. But don't expect me to rollover when it comes to golf. Us ballplayers always play to win.

FREEDOM TO COACH

In 2003 I was hired to manage the Florence Freedom, part of the independent Frontier League. It was a quick hire. Former teammate Chris Sabo resigned from the position right before the start of the season, and they offered me the job just a week before the opener.

It was my first time on the other side of the lines, but once I put on the uniform, I knew it was for me.

By league rules, no player could be older than 27. There were some hidden treasures to be found in the league, but for the most part, I was managing guys who fell just short of what it took to play ball on the highest levels. So I had one thing in mind: making these guys the absolute best players they could be.

Although they didn't always have the skills needed, many of these guys had the confidence. They felt they had been unjustly passed over or released by their old teams, and they were out to prove them wrong. When many others would have given up on their dreams and moved on, these guys were committed to making it. They were hungry and anxious to improve. It was just so refreshing to be around kids like that.

I got a great sense of pleasure when they picked my brain and I could share the lessons I learned from my playing days.

However, the absolute toughest part of the job was crushing these kids' hopes. There's nothing more difficult than telling a kid he just isn't good enough to fulfill his own dream.

I had one kid, a left-handed pitcher, who was just outstanding in my first year as the manager. He was one of the best pitchers in the league. The next season, though, he did a complete turnaround. It was a night-and-day difference, and we just couldn't keep him around anymore. I had to call him into my office and tell him his dream was over. I just felt for the kid so much. I hated it. I hated that part of the job.

I was probably pretty close to being on the other side of that conversation at a few times in my career. I could relate to the kid, and I hated being in the position to tell him he wasn't good enough.

But as tough as that was, I still knew the good outweighed the bad. I knew that for every dream that was crushed, many more were sustained. I even had three or four guys signed out of the league and make it to the minor leagues. Only becoming a father provided a more satisfying feeling.

The Florence Freedom, though, were plagued by management and financial problems, and I was out as head coach a year and a half into it. New ownership has completely turned around the franchise since then, but my time there is over.

I have no hard feelings, though. If anything, I'm thankful I was given the opportunity. It just reaffirmed my desire to return to the game and help tomorrow's players.

Someday, I hope to be back into the bigs for good as a full-time coach or manager. (My stint as a spring training instructor in 2006 is a great start.) Playing for the Cincinnati Reds taught me a lot about the game and how to play it the right way, and I welcome the opportunity to pass along that knowledge to future players.

WORLD SERIES OF GOLF

In 1989 Rick Mahler and I started Baseball's World Series of Golf, an annual golf tournament at Pebble Beach. It's been an event I really look forward to every year, and we've drawn some pretty big names.

Rick, who spent most of his career with the Braves, pitched on Cincinnati's 1990 World Series team, and we became quick friends.

Unfortunately, Rick died of a heart attack in early 2005, but I wanted to keep the golf tournament going. I'm sure Rick would have wanted it that way. Like me, he really enjoyed bringing together baseball people in a fun atmosphere.

We've had a lot of current and former players take part in the event: Paul Molitor, Robin Yount, Bob Horner, Chili Davis, Bud Black, Dave Righetti, George Brett, Ken Caminiti, Jeff Bagwell, and Craig Biggio, among others.

We even get some umpires, such as Bruce Froemming. Bruce was one of the best in the business, but I used to scream at him all of the time back in my playing days.

"All right, Browning," he warned me during his first tournament. "You can't yell at me out here. We're not playing baseball."

I assured him everyone was there just to have fun.

He joined Ed Montague, Gary Darling, my good friend Randy Marsh, and many other umpires throughout the years.

You spend time with these guys outside baseball, and you understand just how great, honest, and genuine these people are.

The thing I cherish more than anything else in baseball is the friendships and camaraderie I developed not only with my teammates, but throughout all of baseball. It's truly a fraternity. There's a bond there that you can't see, but it's there.

When you run across fellow players at card shows or golf tournaments or other events, you always have something in common. You can talk about players and managers and your favorite coaches. You can talk about the hardest throwers or the toughest guys to strike out, your favorite victories and the funniest teammates.

There will always be that common ground that brings you together. As our little golf tournament has shown year after year, baseball really does provide a lifetime of friends.

PETE COMES CLEAN

In early 2004, Pete Rose released his book and admitted that he did, in fact, bet on baseball.

I know a lot of fans probably felt a sense of relief when the news came out. I know some people held out hope that he was actually innocent of betting on baseball, but I think most people knew he was guilty. Those people also knew that the sooner Pete admitted his mistakes, the sooner he might be removed from Major League Baseball's ineligible list.

Personally, I was a little disappointed in the news. I wasn't disappointed that he admitted he bet on baseball. I was just disappointed that I had to find out like everyone else—during his public-relations campaign for his new book.

I had always held onto some small hope that maybe Pete didn't bet on baseball, so I supported him fully in the years after he was banned from the game. I tried to champion his goal of getting into the Hall of Fame, and even during the closing ceremonies at Cinergy Field in 2002, I made sure he got his due acknowledgment. A simple phone call giving me a heads-up on his confession would have meant a lot, but I guess Pete just had a lot going on.

But I was also disappointed in the way Pete went about releasing the news. Whether it was intentional or not, the whole event seemed like a marketing ploy. It just didn't seem sincere, and it obviously did a lot more harm than good. Just when it looked like Pete might get a second chance from baseball, he released his confession in what seemed like another way to make a quick buck.

I suppose, though, that Pete didn't really owe me anything. We didn't really stay in contact after he left the game, except for the softball game in 2002. But I think there was always that mutual respect, so it was saddening to see the whole thing play out.

No matter what happens with Pete in the future, I'll always remember him as a good friend and my favorite manager. Like everyone else, he has faults, but those won't cloud all the wonderful memories I have of the years we spent together.

13

WHEN THE HALL CALLED

WIRE TO WIRE AGAIN

Once the announcement came in December 2005 that I was voted into the Reds Hall of Fame (with Tom Seaver and Lee May), I headed to Great American Ball Park for a small press conference with the local baseball writers.

One of the first comments came from *Dayton Daily News'* Hal McCoy, one of my favorite old-school scribes.

"So, you led the voting from beginning to end," he said, almost like he was prodding for a specific response.

Hal always had a way of steering you into the comment he wanted, so I knew exactly what he was fishing for.

"Yeah, wire to wire, huh?" I joked.

Hal laughed along with me. We knew each other too well.

That phrase *wire to wire* will always hold a special place in my heart, and Hal knew it. Wire to wire has become the moniker for our 1990 season, when we led the standings every day of the year. It was, without a doubt, the most enjoyable season of baseball I've ever experienced. Not just because we won the whole damn thing, but also because I got to enjoy it with so many great teammates.

When I look back on my career—my *Hall of Fame* career now, isn't it?—nothing sticks out more than that championship season. No personal accolade could ever match the excitement, satisfaction, or camaraderie that I experienced in 1990.

I throw a few pitches in the Cincinnati Reds Hall of Fame and Museum. (It was mostly off-speed stuff.) *Photo courtesy of the Cincinnati Reds*

But to be honest, induction into the Reds Hall of Fame comes pretty close. It's another wire-to-wire achievement I'll always cherish.

WHEN THE HALL (LITERALLY) CALLED

If you ask Greg Rhodes, the Reds Hall of Fame executive director, he'll probably tell you that I sounded like the most ungrateful player he ever welcomed to the Reds Hall of Fame. But it was just a big miscommunication.

Dann Stupp, an employee in the Reds creative services department and the coauthor of this book, worked with MLB.com to distribute the updated vote count to the Reds Hall of Fame and the team's media relations department each week. It was part of his regular job responsibilities.

The voting was going on while Dann and I were finishing up the book, so during our weekly meetings, he would let me know where I stood in the standings. Those results were sent out to the public each week, so it wasn't exactly top-secret information.

On the last day of voting, Dann gave me a call and congratulated me on winning the election. He had just gotten the final vote count from MLB.com, and he said that Tom Seaver and I were the winners (Lee May would later be voted in by a veterans committee). I was obviously thrilled and celebrated accordingly that weekend.

A few days later, Greg Rhodes called me at home.

"Congratulations on winning the election," he said. "You're a Hall of Famer."

"Yeah, thanks," I said. "So what'd you need, Greg?"

"Uh, nothing," he said. "That was it."

Greg must have been stumped. He was probably wondering why I wasn't jumping up and down on the other side of the phone. Unfortunately, he didn't know that Dann had already leaked the news. And I didn't know that Dann hadn't told Greg he had already told me.

We all got a big laugh out of it once we got it straightened out. And I reassured Greg that the honor meant everything he expected it would to me.

THANKS TO THE FANS

Leading every day of the Hall of Fame voting was a pretty humbling experience. My good friends Eric Davis and Jose Rijo narrowly beat me out the year prior, and I was hoping I could make a charge for the 2006 inductions.

Reds fans granted me my wish and cast their votes throughout the month-long balloting in December 2005. It was so exciting to get the weekly vote counts and see my name on the top of the list each time.

By now, you obviously know how much the organization means to me, and to become part of its Hall of Fame means just as much to me as if I were being inducted into Cooperstown.

Back when I played the game, I knew I'd never be the best. But like I always say, I knew I could compete with the best. And as it turns out, I'm being honored as a Hall of Famer with the best.

This would have never happened without the support of Reds fans. I want to thank every one of you who voted me in. I'm eternally grateful to you. It really made a fellow Reds fan's dream come true.

GREAT COMPANY

I just wanted to pay tribute to the guys who came before me and made the Cincinnati Reds one of baseball's most remarkable franchises. I'm truly blessed to find myself on the same list as these other Reds Hall of Famers:

Sparky Anderson, 2000	Gus Bell, 1964
Johnny Bench, 1986	Jack Billingham, 1984
Ewell Blackwell, 1960	Rube Bressler, 1963
Smoky Burgess, 1975	Leo Cardenas, 1981
Clay Carroll, 1980	Gordy Coleman, 1972
Dave Concepcion, 2000	Harry Craft, 1963
Sam Crawford, 1968	Hughie Critz, 1962
Jake Daubert, 1966	Eric Davis, 2005
Paul Derringer, 1958	Pete Donohue, 1964
Bob Ewing, 2001	George Foster, 2003
Lonny Frey, 1961	Warren Giles, 1969
Ival Goodman, 1959	Wayne Granger, 1982
Ken Griffey Sr., 2004	Heinie Groh, 1963
Don Gullett, 2002	Noodles Hahn, 1963
Bubbles Hargrave, 1962	Tommy Helms, 1979
Bob Howsam, 2004	Dummy Hoy, 2003
Fred Hutchinson, 1965	Ted Kluszewski, 1962
Larry Kopf, 1965	Brooks Lawrence, 1976
Ernie Lombardi, 1958	Red Lucas, 1965
Dolf Luque, 1967	Jerry Lynch, 1988
Jim Maloney, 1973	Lee May, 2006
Frank McCormick, 1958	Mike McCormick, 1966
Bill McKechnie, 1967	Roy McMillan, 1971

Bid McPhee, 2002

Billy Myers, 1966

Joe Nuxhall, 1968

Tony Perez, 1998

Wally Post, 1965

Jose Rijo, 2005

Frank Robinson, 1978

Tom Seaver, 2006

Mario Soto, 2001

Johnny Vander Meer, 1958

Billy Werber, 1961

Harry Wright, 2005

Joe Morgan, 1987

Gary Nolan, 1983

Jim O'Toole, 1970

Vada Pinson, 1977

Bob Purkey, 1974

Eppa Rixey, 1959

Edd Roush, 1960

Cy Seymour, 1998

Johnny Temple, 1965

Bucky Walters, 1958

Will White, 2004

George Wright, 2005

(The date represents the player's year of induction into the Reds Hall of Fame, which was established in 1958. It's the oldest continually operating team Hall of Fame in baseball.)